KU-522-562

Great Expectations

CHARLES DICKENS

Guide written by

John Mahoney

A *Letts* EXPLORE Literature Guide

First published 1994
Reprinted 1994, 1998
This edition revised by Ron Simpson

Letts Educational
Aldine House
Aldine Place
London W12 8AW
0181 740 2266

Text © John Mahoney and Stewart Martin 1994

Self-test questions devised by Hilary Lissenden

Typeset by Jordan Publishing Design

Text design Jonathan Barnard

Text illustrations Hugh Marshall

Cover illustration Ivan Allen

Design © BPP (Letts Educational) Ltd

Acknowledgements
Outline answers are solely the responsibility of the author, and are not supplied
or approved by the Exam Board.

British Library Cataloguing in Publication Data
A CIP record for this book is available from the British Library

ISBN 1 85758 255 1

Printed and bound in Great Britain

Ashford Colour Press, Gosport, Hampshire

Letts Educational is the trading name of BPP (Letts Educational) Ltd

Contents

Plot synopsis

The story opens on the marshes of the Hoo Peninsular in Kent. Pip, a young boy, helps an escaped convict named Magwitch. Later, Pip is taken to play at Satis House and there he meets the mysterious Miss Havisham in her dilapidated mansion. When Pip is told he has a secret benefactor who is to pay for his being turned into a 'gentleman', he wrongly assumes that his benefactor is Miss Havisham. This news, together with his association with Miss Havisham and her beautiful ward Estella, begin to turn him against his friend and guardian Joe Gargery, the blacksmith, whom he now considers 'beneath' him.

Transported to London to learn to be a gentleman, Pip leads a selfish life and neglects his friends back in the marshes. He pursues a hopeless love for Estella and is fortunate enough to make friends with Herbert Pocket. Herbert is a real gentleman and has a good influence on Pip. The return of Magwitch, the convict, helps Pip to unravel the various mysteries that have surrounded him. He discovers that Magwitch, not Miss Havisham, provided the money for his good prospects. He also learns that Molly, Jaggers' housekeeper, and Magwitch are Estella's parents.

Helping Magwitch to escape downriver, Pip is pursued by an old enemy of Magwitch, Compeyson, who was the man who broke Miss Havisham's heart. In the ensuing fight between Magwitch and Compeyson, Compeyson is killed and Magwitch is arrested. However, Magwitch dies before he can be brought to trial.

Pip, a wiser man and now a true gentleman, is reconciled to Joe. He meets with Estella, whose husband has been killed in an accident, and they look to a future together.

■ Who's who in *Great Expectations*

Pip

Of all the characters in the novel, Pip is the one who develops most. You must be able to identify the stages in his transition from a 'small bundle of shivers' to a mature man with a strong sense of loyalty, justice and honesty. His role as narrator is of fundamental importance to the way we learn about him and his companions.

As a child he is intelligent, imaginative and eager for knowledge, but also sensitive, timid and guilt-ridden. His contacts with Miss Havisham and Estella, and his 'great expectations' create a dissatisfaction which leads to the snobbery and false moral values which threaten to outweigh his finer instincts. It is because he is, in a sense, a victim of immaturity, coincidence and romantic illusion that he retains the sympathy of the reader. When the basis of his pretensions is undermined, he begins to move towards a moral strength which shows respect and love for his fellow man, regardless of social standing and prestige.

At the end of the novel the mature Pip, though a redeemed character, seems to be a wiser and sadder man who shows only a modest optimism about the future.

Joe Gargery

Joe, the good-natured countryman and village blacksmith, is a character who is gradually revealed to the reader. At first he appears kindly but weak in his relationships with Mrs Joe, Pumblechook and Miss Havisham. But his responses to events throughout the novel show his humanity, strength, intelligent tact, unselfishness, complete integrity and lack of pretension.

Nevertheless, one can imagine how embarrassing Pip must sometimes find Joe's habits and manners. Joe provides comic moments with his attempts to express himself and is too admirable a figure to be pitied. At the end of the novel,

Joe emerges as a figure Pip fully respects. He also provides a lesson that social status and money have nothing whatever to do with real worth or being a true gentleman.

Miss Havisham

Fantastic and eccentric, Miss Havisham presides in isolation over her macabre house. The images of decay and death which surround her give clues to the kind of influence she has on Pip and Estella. She instils in Estella an attitude towards men that will cause her great unhappiness, and in Pip expectations which are cruelly false. She comes near to ruining both their lives before she finally realises the enormity of her actions.

She no longer lives in the real world, as is shown by the stopped clocks, the decomposed wedding feast and her mouldering wedding dress. Her melodramatic death is an appropriate end to the life she has led. Her money brings her unhappiness, and even the power it gives her over Pip and Estella eventually comes to nothing.

Estella

Estella, Miss Havisham's adopted daughter, is used by her to take revenge on men. She is brought up to be coldly indifferent to human feelings and to break men's hearts. Her name comes from the Latin word for star, and, like a star, she remains cold and distant, despite Pip's attempts to get close to her. Is there a spark of humanity in Estella? If not, why does she keep warning Pip against falling in love with her?

The effect of Estella's upbringing rebounds on Miss Havisham when she finds Estella has no love for her. It is implied that her marriage to the cruel Drummle softens her, but you may feel that this redemption, undeveloped in the narrative, remains unconvincing.

Magwitch

Also known as Provis and Campbell, the convict Magwitch is another of the story's orphans. At the beginning he is an object of terror for Pip, but his decision to take the blame for the theft of the pie and file shows his sensitivity. By the time he returns to see 'his gentleman' he has become the key to the mysteries surrounding Pip's wealth and the parentage of Estella. At the final stage of the novel, he has changed from being an object of revulsion to someone whom Pip pities and loves.

When we know more of his origins we can have some sympathy for Magwitch, but he is no passive victim of society – as may be seen when he seeks revenge against Compeyson, and eventually kills him. By the time of his trial and death he has acquired a dignity which did not seem to be evident when he was the animal which 'glared and growled' and frightened Pip half to death at the beginning of the novel.

Mrs Joe

Aggressive, domineering and unloving, Mrs Joe glories in martyrdom whilst displaying a degree of social pretension. She is responsible for much of Pip's insecurity and guilt. A cane nicknamed Tickler and a vicious tongue are her instruments of punishment.

Mrs Joe's lingering death after a violent attack by Orlick enables Biddy and Joe to become closer. Does Mrs Joe's long illness create any sympathetic response in the reader? Can you see that to an extent she parallels Miss Havisham in her influence on Pip? In her illness and death does she also, like Miss Havisham, ask forgiveness of the people she has wronged: Orlick, Joe and Pip?

Biddy

Biddy represents 'real woman', in contrast to Pip's fantasy of Estella. Pip uses Biddy as a confidante because she is wise, patient and warm-hearted. She is also truthful, realistic, and is prepared to reproach Pip for his insensitivity (see Chapters 17, 19 and 35). Look for evidence of her feelings for Pip – feelings of which he seems unaware.

Biddy puts into words the moral values that Joe represents but cannot successfully articulate. She is also an orphan but, unlike many of the other orphans in the novel, she does not appear to be ambitious.

Herbert Pocket

Herbert represents the combination of the social and moral qualities of a true gentleman. He is honest yet tactful, socially aware but no snob and, most important, a true and loyal friend to Pip. His success in business is created by 'cheerful industry'.

Herbert provides a good example of Dickens' ability to create comic characters who are also worthy exemplars of noble behaviour: you can doubtless think of at least one other in this novel. Herbert's first appearance (the fight at Satis House) is farcical and elements of the ridiculous re-appear from time to time, but he proves resourceful and courageous as well as thoroughly amiable and gentlemanly.

Jaggers

Jaggers is the formidable but much-respected lawyer who is the key figure in the mystery surrounding Pip. His determination to keep what he knows to himself, neither to confirm nor deny anything, is essential to the plot. He knows the secret of Estella's mother and administers Miss Havisham's plans for Estella. He is also Magwitch's agent and implements his plans for Pip. He is, therefore, a link between all parties. Does he know that Estella is Magwitch's daughter?

The seemingly cold and dispassionate way in which he carries out his professional responsibilities seems to embody the essence of the Victorian legal system. His character is never fully revealed.

Pumblechook

It is fitting that Mrs Joe appropriates Pumblechook, although he is really Joe's uncle, as his self-important bullying of the young is much more her style than that of her mild and tolerant husband. Pumblechook is a prosperous corn-chandler whose every act is dictated by an exaggerated sense of his own position. Within the Gargery household his wealth gives him the status that he craves and he victimises Pip with endless sums, lectures on his low moral state and (later) inflated claims to be his benefactor.

Though often a comic character, Pumblechook is the subject of some vicious satire by Dickens. Several scenes place him embarrassingly outside his class (scorned by Miss Havisham, put in his place by the adult Pip) and Pip as narrator frequently applies words like 'swindling' and 'impostor' to him.

Compeyson

Compeyson is the man who jilted Miss Havisham on her wedding day after embezzling large amounts of her money. He was responsible for leading Magwitch into major crime, but, because of his gentlemanly appearance and plausible tongue, he got off with a lighter sentence than Magwitch when they were on trial for the same crime. He appears only briefly in the novel (Chapters 3, 5, and 47) but his baleful influence permeates the lives of both Magwitch and Miss Havisham.

Orlick

It is worth comparing Orlick with Drummle. Both are physically large and loutish, and though Orlick does not aspire to be a gentleman he does show considerable interest in Biddy. His insolence, brutishness and savagery, especially in his attacks on Mrs Joe and Pip, are his most memorable characteristics.

Bentley Drummle

Bentley Drummle is one of the examples we are given of a 'gentleman'. His expectation is of a baronetcy to which only an accident of birth entitles him – he doesn't otherwise merit it, nor the respect which would go with it. His gracelessness and surly, arrogant manner sets him in sharp contrast with both Herbert and Pip. He is an obvious example of the lesson that money and class do not automatically make a gentleman.

If Pip had married Estella, do you think he would have been able to overcome the distorted view of life which Miss Havisham had instilled in her? Did it need Drummle to make her suffer and return her to a normal human perspective on life – one with which she could more easily respond to Pip's love? Certainly, she was unable to break Drummle's spirit and so fulfil Miss Havisham's plan to take her revenge on men. Only a fatal accident on a horse he had mistreated was able to destroy his brutish life.

Themes and images in *Great Expectations*

Expectations

Expectations

It would be a mistake to see Pip as the only character who has 'great expectations'. Indeed, his expectations and his desire to become a gentleman flow directly from the expectations of others, in particular Magwitch, who makes a fortune with the intention of using his money to turn Pip into a gentleman. Magwitch's plans for the social elevation of Pip are paralleled by those of Miss Havisham, whose overwhelming desire is to take revenge on the breed of 'gentlemen' who so brutally destroyed her hopes and expectations. She plans to do this by turning Estella into a bewitching temptress of men whose beauty hides a hard and unloving heart. Fortunately, both Miss Havisham and Magwitch fail to turn their respective protégé(e)s into the people they had in mind.

Pip's ambitions and their effects are echoed by the aspirations and ambitions of numerous other characters. Herbert Pocket is an obvious model for Pip in Pip's aspirations to become a gentleman. Bentley Drummle provides a sharp contrast with Herbert. The real 'gentle man' of the novel, Joe Gargery, whose only desire is to do what's right by those around him, provides a stark contrast to the scheming and conniving of other characters. He exemplifies qualities of the 'gentle Christian man' against which you can measure other characters.

As you read the novel you should consider what it is that characters like Pumblechook, Wopsle, Orlick and the Pockets aspire to. Does Mrs Joe have any expectations, or Jaggers and Wemmick? And what about the mass of people who frequent Little Britain and haunt Jaggers' office? What are their expectations?

A major feature of many of the characters' aspirations is the acquisition of wealth. Wemmick's concern to lay hands on 'portable property' is one example, and Pip's aspiration to become a gentleman is fuelled by his expectation of coming into great wealth. However, Pip's pleasure in his new-found wealth is cut short when he discovers its true source – and he fails to follow Wemmick's injunction to acquire Magwitch's 'portable property' (Magwitch's notebook containing the details and deeds of his fortune). Ironically, in failing to acquire this easily won wealth, Pip undergoes the change which will enable him to become a true gentleman – can you see how?

Joe's attitude to money is very clear. He willingly accepts the money due to him for the apprenticeship of Pip, but rejects the bribe offered by Jaggers to release him so that Pip might pursue his ambitions. Perhaps he feels that the money Pip is given by the mysterious benefactor is a barrier between them, because of the change it brings about in Pip. Study the other characters' attitudes to money and wealth, the uses they put it to and the opportunities which lack of money denies them.

The acquisition of wealth is clearly associated in Pip's mind with the status of 'gentleman'. Within a short time he is elevated from blacksmith's boy to a young 'gentleman' with 'great expectations'. The lure of money and the prospect of marrying a girl of education and 'breeding' lead Pip to adopt a lifestyle which does not resemble that of a true gentleman. His smart wardrobe, his acquisition of a servant, his feeling that Joe is not suitable company for him in London, his anguish at Magwitch's table manners, all highlight the false understanding he has of what makes a gentleman.

The question 'what is a gentleman?' is central to the novel's concerns and therefore to Pip's expectations. Drummle was born to be a 'gentleman', but isn't one – why? Herbert Pocket has both the temperament and breeding of a 'gentleman', but has no money and little in the way of real prospects – does that make him less of a 'gentleman'? The snobbery of various characters is a feature of a mistaken view of gentility and one that Pip is very much guilty of in his attitude towards Joe. The gradual changes that occur in Pip's character enable us to follow his emerging awareness of what actually makes a 'gentleman' and finally provide the answer to the question: 'can Pip become a real gentleman?'

A particular feature of Pip's life is the feeling of guilt which connects various strands of his life: guilt for the theft of food and a file for Magwitch; guilt for his lies about what happens at Satis House; guilt for his rejection of Joe in the middle parts of the novel. It is Magwitch who provides the money to turn him into a 'gentleman'. It is Miss Havisham who falsely nurtures his desires to love Estella and become a 'gentleman'. It is Joe who is a nagging reminder of Pip's conscience.

Redemption for Pip comes only when he has learned the true values of love, friendship and money, and the falseness of social aspirations, pretensions and snobbishness. He is, in fact, redeemed when he becomes a true 'gentleman' and gives back to Magwitch all that Magwitch hoped for, as well as the news that his daughter is alive and loved by Pip. To Miss Havisham he gives forgiveness and comfort at the end of a bitter life. To Joe he gives the joy of knowing that his Pip is a true 'gentleman' at last.

Structure

Structure

The novel is constructed in three clear parts, each originally a separate volume: nineteen chapters in the first part and twenty chapters in each of the next two. These cover respectively Pip's boyhood, youth and maturity. Close examination of the aspects of suspense and mystery in the novel identifies thirty-six weekly instalments, the form in which the novel first appeared. These are not always identified by the editors of the various published editions.

Dickens uses the format of the traditional fairy tale to tell his story; you may recognise stories in which the poor little orphan sets out to make his fortune in the great city. But here the orphan does not make his fortune (though that is what Pip sets out to do). Instead, Dickens shows the moral development of his hero in the face of a sudden acquisition and subsequent loss of a fortune. Pip's discovery of his real benefactor and his associated loss of fortune result in his moral and psychological growth.

There are other parallels with fairy stories, but again the author has changed the traditional pattern of events. The 'evil and frightening old man', Magwitch, turns out to be Pip's caring benefactor. The 'kindly old grandmother', Miss

Havisham, turns out to be a vindictive old woman, and the 'beautiful princess', Estella, is a cold, almost inhuman figure. The ordinary perceptions of good and evil are, to an extent, obscured in Pip's desire to acquire the status of 'gentleman', and it is some time before he is able to make a clear distinction between the appearances of things and people, and their reality.

Social aspects

This novel is not just a story of Pip and his expectations. It is also a commentary on the society of Dickens' time. Dickens is partly an observer and analyst of society, and partly a moralist speaking about standards of right and wrong. In looking at his view of the criminal world, you should be aware of the author's concerns. He never says Magwitch is a victim of society or that the prisons are filled with people who are there as result of their experiences of an unjust, class-divided society, yet the implications are there and the call for reform is presented as if intended to awaken public conscience.

Throughout the novel, Dickens implies his personal condemnation of an inhuman legal system. He demonstrates this through Magwitch's story, Jaggers' cold professionalism, the scenes in Newgate and the trial. In *Great Expectations* the 'gentleman criminal' Compeyson is given a lighter sentence than Magwitch because of his social class, although in reality his is the greater crime. The ability to pay for a good defence is often more important than guilt or innocence, and Jaggers' skill at manipulating the law is one that not everyone can afford. One of the great ironies of the novel is that Pip's expectations are dependent upon a criminal's money.

Education figures as a theme in this novel in two ways: those passages which talk of the formal process of learning in the cases of Biddy and Pip, and those which reflect on the problems caused by a lack of learning – in the cases of Joe and Magwitch. We are better able to understand Pip because of his mis-education by Mrs Joe, Miss Havisham and Pumblechook, and we sympathise with his efforts to cope with his sudden advancement in society.

The social theme of the novel arises from the interaction of Pip with the other characters, ranging from the working man Joe, to the leisured Finches and the rich Miss Havisham. In this way the reader sees that the influences working on Pip are typical of the society in which he lives.

Atmosphere

Atmosphere

Dickens' descriptive mastery can be observed in the settings he chooses. The landscape in this novel changes as Pip travels up river from the misty marshes and village of his childhood to London, the capital city. Pip waits for his expectations to flower in settings which are generally depressing. Note how his fortunes also seem to follow the ebb and flow of the River Thames: the river brings Magwitch to Pip, drowns Compeyson and is the scene of Magwitch's fatal injuries.

The descriptive powers of Dickens are seen at their best in the marshes, the river and the city landscapes which set the atmosphere surrounding the slowly changing and maturing Pip. The marsh, with its mists and mystery, reflects the mood of Pip's early childhood. It is only when Pip comes to terms with himself that he can finally return to the misty wastes of his childhood and find himself again.

Essays/Examiner's tip icon

This icon is used to draw attention to a section of the **Text commentary** that is particularly relevant to either the section on **How to write a coursework essay** or to the section on **How to write an examination essay**. Each time it is used, a note identifies which section it relates to and adds a comment, quotation or piece of advice.

■ Understanding the relationships

Miss Havisham and Compeyson

Miss Havisham had a half-brother, Arthur, a dissolute and unreliable character. He introduced her to Compeyson, a 'gentleman' swindler. Compeyson became her fiancé, tricked her out of a small fortune and jilted her on the day of her marriage.

Compeyson and Magwitch

Compeyson, by chance, had become acquainted with Magwitch, a petty criminal, and inveigled him into a life of more serious crime. Caught, they were tried, but Compeyson caused Magwitch to be blamed for 'leading the gentleman Compeyson' astray, and Magwitch received the greater sentence – hence his hatred for Compeyson.

Magwitch and Molly

Magwitch and Molly had a daughter called Estella. Molly, charged with murdering another woman, was acquitted, but found herself bound to Jaggers, the lawyer who defended her, on condition that her daughter was given the chance of a better life by being brought up by one of his rich clients, Miss Havisham. Magwitch believes that Molly has also killed their daughter.

Jaggers

Jaggers, a lawyer, acts for Miss Havisham, defended Molly, is known to Magwitch and acts as Magwitch's agent with Pip. He does not know that Estella is Magwitch's daughter.

■ Text commentary

> *Great Expectations* was originally published in 36 weekly parts in a journal called *All the Year Round*, then in a three-volume format. Some modern editions number the chapters from 1 to 59, some number independently within each of the original three volumes. This guide follows the former course, but by placing **Self-test questions** at the end of each volume, makes it possible for readers to adjust to either format.

Chapter 1

In a bleak churchyard, set in the marshlands of the Thames estuary, stands Pip, contemplating his family's graves. A desperately hungry, manacled convict terrorises him. Pip promises to return next morning with a file to cut his chains, and food.

Pip's origins

Pip

The book's introduction presents us with the depressing picture of Pip's origins: he is an orphan who has christened himself 'Pip'. Pip (a seed) is perhaps an appropriate name for someone, here aged seven, whose fortunes we shall follow as he grows to maturity. At the start, Pip is just 'a small bundle of shivers'. Study the stages that he passes through on his way to becoming a mature businessman at the end of the novel.

Pip's early impression of 'the identity of things' leads him to search for his own identity, shown in the sentence beginning 'At such a time...'. This search underlies Pip's ambition to become a gentleman. The bleakness of the marsh landscape matches the mood created by our knowledge of Pip's comfortless past. Pip's isolation is stressed by the long list of his dead relatives – his mother and father and his five brothers.

Childhood

The opening pages of the novel provide a justly celebrated picture of a child's eye view of the world: first the attempts to interpret the tombstone, then the overpowering landscape, and finally the sudden eruption of the 'terrible voice' of the 'fearful man'.

A threatening prospect

Notice how Pip feels threatened by the landscape. The 'low leaden line' (the

river) and the 'distant savage lair' (the sea) prepare us for the appearance of a frightening 'monster' who will soon turn Pip's life upside-down.

The marsh is an important presence in the novel. At this moment it is not a place that Pip finds easy to come to terms with. Its appearance is unfriendly and threatening, and enhances the grim mood of the novel's opening.

Atmosphere

Magwitch and a 'small bundle of shivers'

It does not take much imagination to appreciate the frightening effect of the convict's sudden appearance on Pip. This 'small bundle of shivers' is already frightened by the landscape and, starting to cry from sheer mental and physical desolation, he is terrified half to death by the sudden appearance of the convict.

Magwitch

Characterisation

Magwitch is a character who illustrates Dickens' remarkable power of characterisation. He appears as a terrifying grotesque (physically violent, making bizarre threats: 'I'll have your heart and liver out') and undergoes a steady humanising process until he meets his death nobly.

Despite his sudden and fearful appearance, the human personality of the convict begins to show during the dialogue which follows. The grim humour which accompanies his inquisition of Pip belies his horrendous appearance and threatening behaviour. It also helps to relieve the gloom of the opening and, at the same time, presents a complete contrast to Pip's mood.

Note the stark imagery of a landscape reduced to thin red and black lines. Do they suggest darkness and blood? Certainly the gibbet and the image of a convict limping towards it carry a powerful suggestion of impending doom.

Joe the blacksmith

The fortuitous nature of Joe's profession enables the story to develop smoothly. Pip gets his first set of instructions from the convict which will result in him lying to Joe and stealing from his sister. Later, in fulfilling Magwitch's second set of desires, Pip will neglect Joe in an insensitive and selfish way.

Joe Gargery

Chapter 2

At the village forge, Pip's home, Joe Gargery tells Pip that Mrs Joe is on 'the rampage' with 'Tickler', the punishment cane. Pip conceals his bread in order to take it to the convict, but is dosed with tar water for eating his food too quickly. Guns are heard during the evening, signalling the escape of a prisoner from the prison ships. Pip rises at dawn and steals food and a file in order to avoid the retribution threatened by the convict who is hiding out in the marshes.

Brought up 'by hand'

The phrase 'by hand' usually implies care and love, but in Mrs Joe's case it means the very opposite. It makes one wonder what sort of a man Joe is – a

blacksmith 'brought up by hand'! Note Pip's assessment of Joe: 'foolish, dear fellow'. Your view of him needs to be a little more perceptive. This description of Joe should be kept in mind in order to see to what extent it can be justified by later events. A 'dear fellow' he certainly seems to be, but whether he is 'foolish' remains to be seen.

Mrs Joe revealed

Mrs Joe's character is described here. Does she change during the course of the novel? Notice that she shows no signs of motherliness – the pins and needles at her bib do not make it a comforting place to lay one's head, nor does she show the usual qualities of a loving wife. Perhaps the lack of a first (Christian) name makes her seem a little inhuman.

Mrs Joe's rough treatment and verbal abuse of Joe show the ferocity of her temper and make us sympathetic to Pip's experience of life in her care.

Joe the blacksmith

As you read the novel, note Joe's warmth of spirit. The forge and his fireside seat in the cottage are symbols of his strength and security. Look in this chapter for examples of the bond which exists between Joe and Pip at this point in Pip's life.

A return to the marshes

This chapter marks the end of the first part of the serialised version of *Great Expectations*, and ends on a note of suspense, as Pip makes for the marshes and his appointed meeting with the convict.

Chapter 3

Pip approaches a figure on the misty marsh, but discovers a different man, one with a scar on his face. Pip meets 'his' convict and, when he tells him about the other man, the convict flares up and files furiously at his leg-irons whilst Pip slips away, hardly noticed.

Pip's guilt

Pip

Guilt lies heavily on Pip's conscience. This sense of guilt will stay with him for much of the story. You should be aware of the stages through which he passes as he comes to terms with his actions and the guilt that may attached to them.

Childhood

Pip's guilt is part of his attempt to make sense of the world around him. In these chapters of early boyhood (Dickens wrote that he is 'about 7'), he is subjected to influences and counter-influences: all that he is truly certain of is his sympathy (encouraged by Joe) for the convict's sufferings.

Another convict

The more polite tone of this conversation between Pip and the convict helps to balance the previous frightening meeting. It shows the convict in a quite different light, as someone the reader could perhaps pity.

His response to the news of the other convict, however, is alarming. It suggests that there is no love lost between the two men, and creates mystery. It also provides the diversion which Pip needs to slip off into the mist and return home.

Chapter 4

Christmas Day is a miserable occasion for Pip as he suffers agonies of guilt, fearing exposure as a thief. Dinner is interrupted by soldiers – a search party – arriving at the forge at the very moment Mrs Joe discovers that her pork pie is missing from the pantry.

This first view of Wopsle should be carefully noted. Wopsle will unintentionally parody Pip's aspirations but, unlike Pip, he does not learn from his experience.

Uncle Pumblechook

Uncle Pumblechook here makes his first appearance. One of Dickens' great grotesque creations, he is full of absurd dignity and self-importance, talking nonsense with every appearance of thinking it great wisdom. He rejoices in the role of benefactor: note in the next chapter he gives the sergeant quantities of wine, apparently forgetting that he made a present of it to Mrs Joe. He is one of several adults to oppress Pip with their emphasis on his worthlessness. Do you find Pumblechook a comic figure here? If so, does he remain so throughout the book, or does the characterisation become more vicious?

Pork pie

The terror which Pip feels as Mrs Joe goes to get the pork pie seems to be at

least as great as the fear which he felt in the presence of the convict. The dinner scene is both humorous and dramatic, and Pip's terrified flight to the door ends the chapter with him being confronted by his worst fears – retribution in the shape of soldiers, and a pair of handcuffs meant, apparently, for him. This is the end of the second serial instalment!

Structure

Chapter 5

Joe mends the handcuffs, which are to be used to secure the escaped convict. Joe takes Pip to follow the hunt and together they watch the two convicts fighting like animals in the marsh mud. Before he is led back to the prison ship, Pip's convict tells them that it was he who stole the food from the forge.

Magwitch recaptured

Notice the contrast between the warmth of the forge and the cold, miserable marshland where the convicts hide.

The reasons for the hostility between the two convicts are not explained,

nor why one should want to 'give up' the other, even at the cost of his own freedom, especially when it is clear that he escaped first and went hunting for the second convict only after Pip had told him of the second escape. (One scene will often have a parallel scene later in the novel. This fight between the two convicts will resume later in the novel but, literally, in much deeper water.)

Structure

The first convict's obvious hatred for the other and his allusion to his determination not to let him 'make a tool of me afresh and again' remains a mystery.

It seems to be at this stage that Pip's convict makes a decision that will have tremendous consequences for Pip. The immediate result of his decision is to exonerate Pip from the suspicion of the theft of food and the file. Notice Joe's humanity: 'poor miserable fellow-creatur'. His acceptance of

Social aspects

the convict as a 'fellow' is in marked contrast to the way the convicts are treated in the boat – growled at 'as if to dogs'.

Chapter 6

Pip decides he will not confide in Joe about his part in the theft of the food because his is afraid Joe will no longer trust him. Mr Pumblechook and Mr Wopsle discuss how the convict might have got into the house.

That Pip does not confide in Joe about his theft is the first indication of the separation that will grow between them. Here it is his feeling of guilt perhaps that stops him talking to Joe; later, his guilt brings him back to his senses and leads him back to Joe.

Chapter 7

It is a year later. Pip wants an education and, with the help of Biddy, he learns the basics at a dame-school. Joe tells about his lack of schooling, his unhappy childhood and his reasons for tolerating Mrs Joe's ill humour. Mrs Joe and Mr Pumblechook return from market full of excitement. They tell Pip he is to visit the grand home of the rich eccentric, Miss Havisham, to 'play'.

Educating Pip

The lack of educational opportunities and the casual nature of such provision

Social aspects

as there was, is seen in this chapter. We also get a our first view of Biddy. As narrator, Pip seems more concerned to concentrate on her appearance than on what she does for him in the way of helping him to learn to read. This foreshadows the mistakes he makes later in the novel when he seems much more concerned with external appearances than internal worth. It is Biddy who, through her teaching, helps him take the first steps towards becoming an educated man.

Joe's history

The history which Joe relates shows us yet another 'fatherless' character. It

Joe Gargery

also reveals something of the social conditions of the time, and begins to give us something of a perspective from which to view Joe and his actions, especially with regard to Mrs Joe and Pip. Study carefully the pages in which Joe explains the underlying ideas and philosophy which guide his actions. You will gain a better understanding of him and of his moral strength.

A new beginning for Pip?

Pip's view of the stars, which he associates with cold and pitiless indifference, is important because it closely reflects the plans that Miss Havisham has for Estella (star) and the men who will be attracted by her beauty.

In this chapter the idea of Pip making his fortune through Miss Havisham is perhaps planted in his mind, preparing the way for those coincidences and deceptions which confirm his belief that she is his benefactor.

Chapter 8

At Satis House, Pip is met by a beautiful but arrogant young girl – Estella, who leads him to meet Miss Havisham. She sits surrounded by decay, dressed in an ancient wedding dress. Estella is disdainful of Pip's common language and working-class clothes and manners. Pip is deeply hurt and ashamed of his humble origins. Before he leaves, he wanders about in the derelict brewery where he 'sees' a figure hanging from a beam; the image is that of Miss Havisham.

Estella, the star

Notice Estella's aloofness and coldness and the way she dismisses

Estella

Pumblechook. Remember that she is roughly the same age as Pip, yet it is difficult to imagine Pip being able to dismiss Pumblechook so easily. It is plain that she has had rather a different upbringing from Pip. The name Estella means 'star' and this is what she resembles as she comes, candle in hand, down the dark passage. Miss Havisham reveals something of her warped plans in her instruction to Estella to 'break his heart'.

Miss Havisham and Satis House

As we explore the house in Pip's company, we soon come to see that, whilst

Miss Havisham

the shell of the building is impressively large, it has no 'heart'. This is equally true of its owner and her name – a pun on 'having' and 'sham' – reflects her physical and psychological state. In terms of wealth she has everything, but it has brought her little happiness or fulfilment.

Pip's description of how Miss Havisham is dressed contains no hint of the terrible reality behind it. The extraordinary state of her clothing says much about her state of mind.

The comparison of Miss Havisham to a waxwork and a skeleton foreshadows her fate. Note the ominous references: 'grave clothes', 'a shroud', 'corpse-like', and the associated images of darkness and decay that surround her – shut curtains, a stopped clock, candles, artificial light. There is no suggestion that she has anything worthwhile to offer Pip, and she begins to take pleasure in watching Estella hurt Pip. We do not yet know why.

A fairy tale

Miss Havisham, a macabre and melodramatic figure in a darkened mansion, casts her blighting spell on Pip through the cold beauty of Estella. Notice the fairy-tale style of presentation: the traditional wicked witch, young hero, beautiful princess and enchanted palace.

Pip, appearances and reality

Estella's snobbish contempt for Pip not only says something about Estella and the way Miss Havisham has brought her up, but also reflects prevailing social attitudes towards the poor and uneducated. Estella gives Pip his food as if he were a disgraced dog. Note how she criticises almost every aspect of Pip's appearance and behaviour, and how deeply he takes these comments to heart. **Social aspects** What does this tell you about Pip's view of himself, his home, and Joe?

Social class

Pip's attempts to rise above his class begin with his exposure to the world of Satis House. It is easy to see why Estella's beauty and cold composure make him ashamed of himself, but Dickens also makes it clear that the distinction is trivial: 'He calls the knaves Jacks, this boy!'

From now until the end of the chapter, Pip analyses himself and his life. His assessment, that he is 'morally timid and very sensitive' and (in the last paragraph of the chapter) that he is a common labouring boy in a 'low-lived bad way', is the beginning of his impatience with Joe and all he stands for. He worries about his appearance, a recurrent theme, and is gradually turning Estella into his 'fairy princess', despite the way she treats him.

Pip

Pip is now effectively launched upon the path he will follow through the novel: he will be led by his love for Estella and by his ambition to be to her equal, both socially and culturally.

Chapter 9

On his return to the forge, Pip is questioned by Mrs Joe and Pumblechook and he invents stories in order to satisfy them. Later he admits to Joe that he lied and tells him that he is aware of being 'common'. Joe is shocked and warns Pip against dishonesty. But Pip is too deeply affected by Estella to be able to shake off his new-found feelings of inferiority.

The easily deceived

Pip's unwillingness to parade Miss Havisham's eccentricity before Mrs Joe and Pumblechook is a mark of his sensitivity: or is it an early hint of snobbery that keeps his new world (especially Estella) separate from the old? The comedy comes from the readiness with which all believe him: Joe innocently ('I believe you! Wonderful!'), the other two complacent in their 'wisdom'. Pumblechook is convinced he knows 'the way to have him': you will easily find evidence to the contrary.

When Pip confesses to Joe that he has lied about his time at Satis House, one can only laugh at Joe's desperate desire to find that there was at least one dog there, even if it was only a puppy, to support Pip's story. The unsettling effect of Pip's visit is plain, but Joe is certain of the value of his own advice: 'if you can't get to be oncommon by going straight, you'll never get to do it by going crooked'.

Chapter 10

Pip asks Biddy to teach him everything she knows. He hopes to become less 'common' by achieving some kind of education. Later he goes to the inn, the Three Jolly Bargemen, to meet Joe. Here he finds Joe and Mr Wopsle in the company of a stranger. This man questions Pip and stirs his drink with a file – the very file Pip gave to the convict. As he leaves, the stranger gives Pip a shilling wrapped in a crumpled paper, which is later found to be two pound notes.

Biddy is induced to help Pip to 'get on in life'. Here is a description of what was known as a 'dame-school' in Victorian England. Notice Pip's realism in the paragraph beginning: 'It appeared to me...', and the fact that despite everything, he determines to persevere with his plan to be properly educated.

The mysterious stranger

Structure

The stranger whom Pip meets in the inn is a reminder of Pip's earlier encounter with Magwitch and indicates that the incident is not yet finished with. This episode is paralleled later, when Pip meets yet another stranger in this same public house. It is not safe to assume that the convict has now, via the stranger, paid his debt of gratitude and disappeared from the story.

Examiner's tip

In examining the theme of 'great expectations' for the question on page 66, note that there are both personal ambition (as in Pip's desire to be worthy of Estella) and transformation imposed from outside. The first sign of this intervention occurs here (the bank-notes) and Pip is full of dread at the link with the convict. How much greater will be his later shock!

Chapter 11

Pip makes a second visit to Miss Havisham. This time there are other visitors in Satis House – Miss Havisham's poor relations. Pip walks with Miss Havisham in a room where there is a huge table still laid with the rotted wedding breakfast. Miss Havisham tells Pip that she expects to be laid out on this table when she is dead. Pip and Estella play cards for Miss Havisham's entertainment, but she gains more pleasure from encouraging Pip to admire Estella's beauty. Estella is again contemptuous of Pip. As Pip wanders in the gardens he meets a 'pale young gentleman' who challenges him to a friendly boxing match, which he loses with good humour. As he leaves, Estella allows Pip to kiss her cheek.

Chance meetings

The chance meeting with the man who turns out to be Jaggers, Miss Havisham's lawyer, later helps to mislead Pip into believing that Miss Havisham is his benefactor. Jaggers will play a very important role in Pip's life. Pip also meets Herbert Pocket, who provides a pleasant contrast to the various 'toadies and humbugs' Pip has just met, and the perverted characters of Miss Havisham and Estella. Herbert's insistence on observing rules, his determination and his refusal to accept defeat are attractive traits and make him a good example for Pip in his search to 'better himself'.

Structure

The various chance meetings set up a series of remarkable coincidences for later in the book: Herbert, of course, takes a quite different role from simply one of Miss Havisham's poor relations, though perhaps the greatest coincidence settles around Estella's parents. These coincidences impose a structure on Pip's life, but how convincing are they? They depend on the role of one key character to link them together: who is that?

Images of decay

The centrepiece of the derelict wedding feast is the great cake. It symbolises those great but disappointed expectations which Miss Havisham once had, and its obscene condition reflects the state of her mind. Her comment that she will be laid on that table when she is dead finds ironic fulfilment later in the novel. In this context, the reference to Pip's anxiety that both he and Estella might 'begin to decay' is also ironic, given Miss Havisham's plans for them.

Atmosphere

As Pip returns home we see a repetition of the black and red image which was characteristic of his meetings with the convict earlier. It perhaps suggests the danger, both moral and physical, which will afflict Pip in the years to come – the fire which the furnace throws across his path seems to be a warning directly from Joe.

Chapter 12

Pip begins to pay regular visits to Miss Havisham's. He wheels her round the darkened rooms and plays cards with Estella, while Miss Havisham mutters maliciously about Estella breaking his heart. Joe is sent for and ordered to bring with him the indentures for Pip to be apprenticed to him as a blacksmith. This causes Mrs Joe and Pumblechook to speculate on Pip's future.

Pip's hopes for greater things through Miss Havisham meet with little encouragement from her. She seems much more concerned to watch the effect Estella is having on him. Her injunction to Estella: 'Break their hearts...no mercy!', is ironic in the light of the quarrel that she and Estella have later.

Chapter 13

Joe is totally confused in Miss Havisham's presence and channels all his conversation through Pip. This embarrasses Pip. Miss Havisham gives Joe twenty-five guineas as Pip's premium and tells them to expect no more from her. Later, Mrs Joe and Pumblechook come to view Pip's apprenticeship as good fortune and there is a celebration dinner at the Blue Boar. Pip does not find the evening enjoyable and is miserable when he contemplates the 'common' nature of a blacksmith's work.

Joe visits Satis House

Despite the embarrassment that Pip feels about Joe's replying through him to Miss Havisham's questions, Miss Havisham herself seems not the least bit put out by it. Note that Joe mentions that he did not expect a premium 'with the boy', but gets one nevertheless. (This episode finds a parallel in a similar conversation with Jaggers, but which has a different outcome.) Pip's embarrassment at Joe is understandable (his conviction that Miss Havisham should know everything that Pip knows is more than naive), but Joe shows his customary rightness of judgement and, later, even an inarticulate cunning in the way that he breaks the news to his wife.

Social class

Dickens, as so often, treads a delicate line here. We cannot but be amused at Joe's lack of social graces and foolish comments ('Which I meantersay, Pip, as I hup and married your sister...' is not the most sensible answer to Miss Havisham on his relationship to Pip), but who can doubt his moral superiority - and, in some ways, greater sense?

Miss Havisham's reaction to Joe shows a shrewd awareness of character on her part. Joe comes away from this encounter with his dignity intact.

There are many characters here whose behaviour is foolish and absurd (Wopsle, for instance, in his most declamatory vein), but at the other extreme from Joe's inarticulate honesty is 'that swindling Pumblechook' who assumes the role of Pip's benefactor and treats Pip like a criminal whom he is saving from his misdeeds.

Chapter 14

Pip recalls how he once looked forward to working alongside Joe at the forge. Now he is obsessed with a feeling of shame about his humble position, and reflects how Estella would despise him if she were to see him at work.

Pip's view of his home has changed, and he is bitterly disappointed about being indentured to Joe. The 'ungracious condition' of Pip's mind at this stage suggests that the unsettling influence of Miss Havisham and Estella is beginning to have its effect on him.

Chapter 15

Pip continues to try to educate himself, but his efforts to help Joe to learn end in failure. Joe agrees, with some reservation, to Pip's taking a half-day holiday in order to visit Miss Havisham. Orlick, Joe's journeyman, resents this favouritism. He insults Mrs Joe, and Joe is obliged to knock him down. Pip visits Miss Havisham. On his return he finds Mrs Joe has been attacked.

Pip resents his style of life

Pip

The fact that Pip does not reveal to Joe his unhappiness about being a blacksmith is one of his redeeming features. Note, however, the reason he tries to help Joe with his education. His determination to visit Miss Havisham gives us some idea of his desperate frame of mind. It is interesting to contrast the Pip we knew before the visits to Satis House with the one we see now.

Childhood

Whatever the worthiness of life at the forge, it would not be enough to make an interesting novel. Now, as years pass, Pip develops a taste for the greater world outside: life at Satis House 'appeared to have something to do with everything that was picturesque.'

Pip clings to his hopes of help from Miss Havisham, but she means it when she says: 'I hope you want nothing? You'll get nothing'. Her evident enjoyment at his discomfiture shows she has not changed. Despite Estella's absence, the visit brings back old memories and intensifies his dissatisfaction with life at the forge.

Mrs Joe is attacked

Orlick's comment that he had followed Pip into town foreshadows the time

Structure

when he will do so again, but that will be to 'London town', and with dangerous intent towards Pip.

Mrs Joe meets a sudden violent attack and suffers a lingering death. The attack and her subsequent death clear the way for Biddy to move into the house and for her relationship with Joe to develop.

The chapter itself is cleverly structured so that the tragedy, though prepared for, is not expected. Despite the fight and the unsatisfactory interview with Miss Havisham, the chapter is notable for a variety of comic incidents. First of all Pip and Joe talk of Miss Havisham's and Joe's conversation is a glorious mixture of shrewdness ('Which her name ain't Estavisham') and nonsense (the inability to realise that Pip did not mean a present by a 'remembrance'). Orlick's character is full of bizarre details, entertaining as well as menacing. Finally we have Wopsle's theatricals (ultimately accompanied by Orlick's rendition of 'Old Clem'). The commotion at the Three Jolly Bargemen shocks the reader no less than it does Pip.

Chapter 16

Pip's suspicions are aroused when a convict's leg iron, which has been filed through, is found near Mrs Joe. The cut is an old one and Pip believes it is his old convict's iron from years before. The police cannot solve the mystery, but Pip suspects Orlick or even the stranger with the file at the Three Jolly Bargemen. Biddy joins the household to care for Pip, Joe and Mrs Joe, now paralysed and unable to speak.

Joe Gargery

Again Pip feels guilty, this time for the attack on Mrs Joe. This gives some idea of the mental turmoil he finds himself in and the lack of security he feels. Bear this in mind when making judgements about his character. The mystery of who attacked Mrs Joe is added to these other mysteries yet to be resolved.

A mystery of a different nature is solved by Biddy when she realises that Mrs Joe wants Orlick's company: there remains the mystery of why she does.

Chapter 17

Pip's apprenticeship continues and he makes yearly visits to Miss Havisham. Biddy gains importance in Pip's life and he confides in her, telling her of Estella and the reason for his wish to become a gentleman. Biddy suggests he should not see life through Estella's eyes and that she is not worthy of his love. Pip says he would do better to fall in love with Biddy but she, a realist, tells him that he never will.

Biddy is concerned that Orlick is attracted to her and Pip feels Joe should dismiss him. Pip's wish to face the future realistically is frustrated by the hope that Miss Havisham will one day make his fortune.

The conversation between Pip and Biddy is interesting. The admiration which he expresses for her is strangely mixed with insensitivity. You should also note that he is very self-absorbed: his every thought is about what he wants. Biddy's analysis of his reasons for wanting to be a 'gentleman' is particularly interesting. His comment about wishing he could make himself fall in love with her is not very tactful.

Chapter 18

Pip is in the fourth year of his apprenticeship. Jaggers, a lawyer from London, arrives at the Three Jolly Bargemen. He informs Pip that he has 'great expectations' but is not, at this stage, to know who his benefactor is. Pip assumes it to be Miss Havisham. He is to leave for London to be educated as a gentleman.

Pip's expectations

Structure

This is the second meeting Pip has had with a stranger in this public house; the other meeting was also related to Magwitch, his real benefactor. This duplication of events helps to provide strong structural links in the novel, and in this case could give a hint as to who really gives Jaggers his instructions in respect of Pip.

Expectations

The news that Pip has 'great expectations', heard from the lips of a man he met at Satis House, convinces Pip (wrongly as it turns out) that Miss Havisham is his benefactress. The strict emphasis on the secrecy that is to surround the source of this money adds another mystery to the novel. Jaggers' determination that Pip should use the absolutely correct words in response to his questions suggests that he is as concerned with the absolute letter of the law as he is with its spirit.

Ultimately Pip will blame himself for his misunderstandings about the source of his 'expectations', but you will note that Jaggers' unwillingness to step outside his instructions helps to mislead Pip. See what examples you can find: what, for instance, is the truth behind Matthew Pocket's appointment as his tutor and what does Pip, quite naturally, assume?

Pip prepares to leave home to become a gentleman. Note Pip's feelings as his departure nears, particularly his growing sense of isolation. You will have noticed his references to needing to avoid 'coarse and common' things.

Chapter 19

Joe burns Pip's indentures and Pip takes a last walk through the familiar places of his childhood. He talks to Biddy about Joe, asking her to improve Joe so that he is fit for a better station in later life. Biddy reminds Pip of Joe's pride and worth. Pip visits Miss Havisham before leaving for London. She has heard from Jaggers of his expectations.

Note the irony of Pip imagining himself bestowing good food on the villagers and of his feelings about the convict – who is the person who would pay for that food! Read his conversation with Biddy about Joe's manners, then his later encounter with Trabb's boy. Pip is already out of touch with the reality of life as it is lived in the marshes.

Pip leaves the marshes

Pip does not wish Joe to see him off in the coach, conscious of the 'difference' that now exists between them. He is in a state of emotional upheaval. The

mist lifts and for a moment he regains the vision of his lost innocence and breaks down. The reader may feel sympathy with Pip at this stage because of the tremendous conflicts that are going on in his mind.

Structure

This chapter marks the end of the first volume and also of the first of three major stages in the novel. Pip's boyhood has come to an end. From enjoying an innocent and loving relationship with Joe, Pip has experienced an emotionally muddled adolescence but has kept sight of a single goal – to become a gentleman.

◼ Self-test questions Chapters 1–19 (Volume 1)

Uncover the plot

Delete two of the alternatives given, to find the correct plot. Beware possible misconceptions and muddles.

Pip, an orphan living with ~~Mr Pumblechook/his uncle~~/his sister, is frightened by an escaped convict/~~a hulk/Mrs Joe~~ into bringing a file and some food to the ~~Battery~~/the churchyard/~~the forge~~. He does so, at first mistaking his convict for another. Christmas dinner is interrupted by a ~~constable/carols~~/soldiers, and Joe and Pip join the hunt for and the arrest of the ~~hulks~~/the escaped prisoners/~~Mr Wopsle~~. Pip is invited to ~~work/to supper~~/to play at Mrs Havisham's/~~Uncle Pumblechook~~'s/~~Biddy's~~ and meets the insulting/~~friendly/plain~~ Estella. Later he calls in at the Three Jolly Bargemen and meets a ~~soldier~~/stranger/~~bargeman~~, who stirs his drink with a ~~pipe/gun~~/file and gives Pip a shilling wrapped in two one-pound notes.

Pip's visits to Miss Havisham become regular. ~~Mrs Joe/Biddy~~/Joe brings Pip's indentures to Satis House and Pip is apprenticed; he is growing increasingly ~~fond/proud~~/ashamed of his home and profession. Joe's ~~uncle/lawyer~~/journeyman Orlick is resentful when Pip takes a holiday to see Miss Havisham – only to learn that Estella is ~~out~~/abroad/~~married~~. Mrs Joe/~~Joe/Orlick~~ is viciously attacked and ~~Biddy/Sarah Pocket~~/Mr Wopsle's great-aunt moves in. Pip confesses his admiration of Estella and his hopes of becoming a ~~blacksmith/lawyer~~/gentleman. Pip learns from Mr Jaggers, ~~a tailor/shopman~~/lawyer, that he has a benefactor from whom he will receive property and an education. Suspecting this benefactor to be Miss Havisham/~~Mr Trabb/Mr Barnwell~~, he leaves for London.

Who? What? When? Why? How?

1   Who was Georgiana?
2   What is stuck in the bib of Mrs Joe's apron?
3   What relationship to Joe is Mr Pumblechook, and what is his profession?
4   Where are the two convicts found, and what are they doing?
5   How is Pip supposed to behave at Miss Havisham's?
6   Where is Miss Havisham's 'other shoe'; how does Pip describe it?
7   Why does Pip profess himself unable to describe Miss Havisham's 'as (his) eyes had seen it'?
8   What does the stranger use to stir his rum-and-water, and why is this of interest to Pip?
9   Who does 'the burly man of an exceedingly dark complexion' that Pip met on Miss Havisham's stairs turn out to be?
10   What is the centrepiece on Miss Havisham's long table?
11   Where does Miss Havisham say she will be laid, and when?
12   Why are Pip and Joe to bring Pip's indentures to Miss Havisham?
13   What Christian name does Joe's journeyman claim?
14   What is Biddy's opinion of Estella, from Pip's words?
15   What are the two main conditions that 'encumber' Pip's expectations?

Who is this?

From your knowledge of the characters in the novel, identify the following people.
1   Who looks like 'a small bundle of shivers'?
2   Who says 'your heart and your liver shall be tore out, roasted and ate'?
3   Who 'made a grab at Tickler, and…Ram-paged out'?

4   Who says, and of whom: 'Whatsume'er the failing on his part, Remember reader he were that good in his hart'?
5   Who says: 'I wish to say something respecting this escape. It may prevent some persons laying under suspicion alonger me'?
6   Who looks like a 'ghastly waxwork' and a skeleton?
7   Who says: 'Well! You can break his heart,' and to whom?
8   Who says of Pip: 'And what coarse hands he has. And what thick boots!'?
9   Who has 'his fishy eyes and mouth open, his sandy hair inquisitively on end, and his waistcoat heaving with windy arithmetic'?
10 Who says: 'If you can't get to be oncommon through going straight, you'll never get to do it through going crooked'?
11 'He seemed so brave and innocent, that although I had not proposed the contest, I felt but a gloomy satisfaction in my victory.'
12 '...a broad-shouldered, loose-limbed, swarthy fellow of great strength.'
13 '...destined never to be on the Rampage again.'
14 '...one of those,...who make the most of every chance.'
15 'May I, as an old friend and well-wisher?'

Familiar themes

What important theme or image in the novel is being developed by the following lines/events?

1   'In his working clothes, Joe was a well-knit, characteristic-looking blacksmith; in his holiday clothes, he was more like a scarecrow in good circumstances...' (4)
2   'Let him make a tool of me afresh and again?' (5)
3   'We don't know what you have done, but we wouldn't have you starved to death for it, poor miserable fellow-creatur...' (5)
4   'Her contempt was so strong, that it became infectious, and I caught it.' (8)
5   '...her light came along the dark passage like a star.' (8)

On the other hand

Find a quote from the text that could be used to counterbalance the following statements.

1   Mrs Joe is a fine figure of a woman. On the other hand, when Pip first describes her, he says...
2   Pip thinks that his convict is a fearful man with no conscience. On the other hand, when he is arrested, the convict says he stole the pie. Why?
3   Joe thinks his father had a good heart. On the other hand, how did he treat Joe's mother?
4   Pip does a terrible thing in lying to Mrs Joe and Pumblechook about his visit to Miss Havisham. On the other hand, he does explain why he felt it necessary...
5   Pip feels ignorant and backward because of how Estella treats him. On the other hand, Joe says that Pip is uncommon in two ways...

Like what?

What/who do the following metaphors/similes describe, and what effect do they achieve?

1   '...the dead wall of her face'
2   '...like the steam-hammer, that can crush a man or pat an egg-shell.'
3   'Brag is a good dog, but Holdfast is better.'
4   'He was throwing his finger at both of us'
5   '...a gallon of condescension'

Chapter 20

Pip arrives in London and goes to Jaggers' office. He observes Jaggers' professional handling of his clients and learns of his own financial arrangements. Pip then goes to Barnard's Inn, where he is to lodge temporarily with Herbert Pocket.

Mr Jaggers, justice and mercy

Pip's dreams of London do not match the reality. His stroll around the city gives him an idea of what London is really like, and a view of the more brutal aspects of the legal system. Note how Jaggers treats those who would be his clients – there isn't much sense of justice and even less of sentiment in his dealings

Social aspects with these people.

You will probably find it difficult to assess how Dickens wishes us to assess Jaggers' character. His dominance and self-assurance are clear enough, but is he a good man? He discharges his duty to Pip conscientiously, he is certainly of assistance to several characters in the novel, his popularity is evident, but how do you respond to incidents like that with Mike, who finds a witness prepared to swear 'in a general way, anythink'? Do we feel that Jaggers is personally corrupt, or is it just part of the satire of the law that so often occurs in Dickens' novels?

Characterisation

With Jaggers, as with many Dickens characters, we find a vivid and convincing set of habits and patterns of conversation, but beneath them he remains a man of mystery. You will find it possible to predict Jaggers' reaction to events, impossible to know his true feelings. You may wonder how far his mystery is deliberately cultivated.

Chapter 21

Wemmick takes Pip to Barnard's Inn, which is shabby and uninviting. Herbert is out when Pip arrives, but on his return welcomes Pip warmly. They recognise each other as the youthful boxers in the garden of Satis House.

Notice the contrast between Pip's high expectations and sordid reality. His 'great expectations' have caused him to exchange the comfort of life with Joe and Biddy and the open landscape of the marshes, for the narrow city streets and the depressing surroundings of Barnard's Inn.

Atmosphere

Pip meets Herbert Pocket again

We immediately see Herbert as a man who would not take anything from his father – he has his 'own bread to earn'. This contrasts with Pip, who finds

Expectations

himself here only because he has been given everything he has by a stranger. Consider how apt the descriptions they give of each other are. Pip cannot comprehend how Herbert could take disappointment lightly, which highlights the great difference between their characters. Why should Herbert's light-hearted and frank explanations of his family connections with Miss Havisham and Mr Jaggers make Pip feel on 'dangerous ground'?

Chapter 22

Herbert and Pip have dinner. Herbert demonstrates tact in helping to correct Pip's table manners. He gives him a nickname – Handel. Pip learns the story of Miss Havisham. Herbert is working in a counting house and has no 'expectations' from Miss Havisham. Herbert takes Pip to Hammersmith where he is to study with Matthew Pocket.

Herbert assesses Estella and defines a 'gentleman'

Herbert accurately assesses Estella's character: 'hard and haughty and capricious' and sums up Miss Havisham's plans for her: 'brought up by Miss Havisham to wreak vengeance on all the male sex'. Read carefully Herbert's account of Miss Havisham's life story and his description of the avaricious nature of most of her relatives. This account is paralleled when later Magwitch's life story is recounted.

Expectations

Notice Herbert's natural tact and friendliness as he agrees to help improve Pip's manners. He provides an example of what a 'true gentleman' should be. Herbert's father's comment that 'a true gentleman in heart' would be 'a true gentleman in manner' is a reminder of Pip's expectations of being a gentleman, and gently points up the misguided view Pip has of what makes one.

Though a model of gentlemanly behaviour, Herbert Pocket is presented in a humorous manner: for example, for his habit of going to the counting-house and 'looking about' himself. His mother is an even more comical figure, with infants tumbling all over her and her dignified, but nonsensical, treatment of Pip: is she also an admirable character like Herbert?

Social class

Mrs Pocket is not impressive as an example of superior breeding, being the daughter of a knight who was nearly a baronet. Her good manners to Pip consist of asking inappropriate questions and continuing her reading. Then, of course, snobbery will always bring the 'toady neighbour', as in Chapter 23.

Chapter 23

At the Pockets' house, Pip meets his fellow students Drummle and Startop. He also learns about the Pocket family. Matthew, though a fine scholar, is hopelessly inadequate in practical matters and his wife is no better. Born of an aristocratic family, she is ineffectual in handling the organisation of their domestic life.

Pip's snobbery

The humorous account of Mrs Pocket's snobbery caricatures the snobbery

Pip

which Pip shows at various times. Pip's desire to add elegance to his rowing style shows his continuing determination to become a 'gentleman'. His reaction to the comment that he has 'the arms of a blacksmith' shows how ashamed he now feels of his background. The introduction of the river to the narrative is important as its image lends continuity to the events of Pip's life.

Chapter 24

Matthew Pocket is an ideal tutor for Pip and plans his education to fit his future life as that of a gentleman of leisure. Pip decides to continue to live with Herbert and consults Jaggers about his allowance. Wemmick, Jaggers' head clerk, takes Pip to see his formidable employer in action in court. He also shows him gifts from condemned criminals which he terms 'portable property', invites him to his Walworth home and tells him to observe Jaggers' housekeeper when he goes to dine at Jagger's house.

Pip the gentleman

Expectations

Pip's education is not to include training for any profession because he is destined to be a 'gentleman'. Compare the characters of Matthew and Joe. Both are childlike in some ways, but both are also gentlemen. Does Pip recognise this, at least so far as Matthew is concerned? Notice Pip's growing confidence in this chapter, even when confronting the formidable Jaggers.

A 'wild beast tamed'

The guided tour of Jaggers' establishment is a timely reminder of the savage

Social aspects

face of justice and the vagaries of its workings. This is hardly real justice at work. The tour establishes a friendly relationship between Wemmick and Pip. Wemmick hints at something very strange about Jaggers' housekeeper – 'a wild beast tamed', though at this stage the reader only recognises this as an illustration of Jaggers' power. You should keep it in mind, though.

Chapter 25

Pip studies in the Pockets' home. His dislike of Drummle grows. He also is faced with the 'Toady' Pockets who fawn upon him because of his new-found wealth. He begins to develop some expensive habits. While visiting Wemmick's 'castle' at Walworth, Pip sees another side of Wemmick, and meets the 'aged parent'.

It is perhaps fortunate that Pip seems able to recognise the unpleasantness of Drummle. His friendships with Herbert and Startop throws light on his own underlying character – he instinctively associates with 'real' gentlemen.

A visit to the 'aged-parent'

The description of Wemmick's home and the extraordinary difference between the public and private Wemmick highlights Wemmick's need to preserve a strict barrier between his two lives, perhaps in order to maintain his sanity. The drawbridge is a particularly apt image of this.

Social aspects
Contrast Wemmick's loving care for his 'aged parent' and Pip's treatment of Joe. It is not quite the same relationship or situation, but is the underlying concept the same? The atmosphere of *Great Expectations* is particularly sunny among Dickens' later novels, despite the fact that tragic and pathetic events abound. One sign of this cheerfulness of tone is the large number of characters who are drawn in such a way as to balance the comically ridiculous and the worthy, characters who either experience no suffering or finally overcome it. Wemmick is one such; see how many more you can think of.

Chapter 26

Jaggers invites Pip and his fellow students to dine. Drummle gets drunk, boasts of his rowing prowess and generally behaves badly. Jaggers takes a great interest in him. Jaggers forces his housekeeper to show her strong wrists. Drummle's behaviour deteriorates. A month later he leaves the Pockets' household.

The argument between the four young men provides some entertainment for Jaggers, particularly Drummle's part in it. Indeed, at one point near the end of the chapter, Jaggers is almost drawn to make a prediction about Drummle's future. Given Jaggers' experience, one wonders what sort of future he sees for him. Note also how the other three display their characters, and the consider the differences between them.

Pip's style of dispute may have too much of the youthful prig about it, but it is at least superior to Drummle's sulks and repetitions: note that Drummle's enmity extends far beyond Pip.

Chapter 27

A letter comes from Biddy saying Joe will visit Pip in London. Pip, snobbishly conscious of Joe's manners, dreads the visit. Joe brings news that Estella has returned to England and wants to see Pip. Joe is awkward, even comical, yet he leaves with dignity, knowing that his presence is an embarrassment to Pip. Pip runs after Joe, but it is too late.

Joe visits London

The letter from Biddy announcing Joe's visit shows her awareness of how Pip might respond to Joe's wish to visit him in London. She suggests that Pip's 'good heart' will counterbalance the fact that he is now a 'gentleman'! When Herbert meets Joe, the reader is presented with an example of truly gentlemanly behaviour. By contrast, all Biddy's fears are confirmed in the way Pip behaves towards Joe.

Dickens' presentation of Joe means that Pip's stiffness towards him is as easy to understand as it is to deplore. His long speech at the end of the chapter contains much homely wisdom as well as generosity of spirit, but you will find no difficulty in building up a list of comically foolish things he says and does: his reaction to being offered tea or coffee or to being asked for his hat might be a good start.

Joe Gargery

In the last paragraph, Pip recognises that what is important about Joe is not his clothes, but the man's quality and 'simple dignity'. Perhaps Pip is beginning to show a greater awareness of the difference between appearance and reality. Look back to the end of Chapter 19 and compare Pip's feelings there.

Chapter 28

While travelling to Satis House, Pip hears a conversation between two convicts who are being transported by coach, under guard. One is the man who gave Pip the two pound notes years before.

Structure

Notice the way Dickens inserts a reminder of Pip's connection with the convicts, particularly Magwitch, just when his future and its connection with Miss Havisham seem beyond question. This makes us wonder whether Magwitch will return at some stage.

Chapter 29

Pip goes to Satis House, believing that Miss Havisham intends him for Estella. Orlick is now porter at the gate. Estella, now a beautiful woman, warns Pip that she has no heart. But he loves her, despite everything, with a romantic passion. Miss Havisham urges him to love Estella utterly. Jaggers dines with them but discloses nothing. Pip's neglect of Joe is evident when he returns to the Blue Boar, rhapsodising over Estella, and fails to visit the forge.

Pip's fairy tale

Pip clearly believes that Miss Havisham has grandiose plans for him, and

indulges in a romantic fantasy, reminding us of the fairy-story style of the novel. He is unable (or is it unwilling) to face reality. His love for Estella he holds to be the sole motivating force for his life. The sight of Orlick as porter, when he has composed himself to face Estella, is a shock to Pip. The deep-rooted hatred they have for each other is obvious and Orlick is clearly a dangerous man, but you will also find humour in his argumentative logic and negative view of the world.

Pip

Pip's failings

Pip's ready agreement with Estella's assumption that he will have changed his

companions since his change of fortunes points to his lack of moral fibre and human judgement, serious faults in his character.

When Miss Havisham draws Pip to her and launches into the extraordinary litany of commands that he should love Estella, effectively against all reason, we suddenly realise how deeply she was wounded by her fiancé's actions.

Miss Havisham

Questions without answers – yet

There are many questions posed in this chapter for the reader. Can you

remember what Herbert told Pip of Miss Havisham's history? Did he mention Estella? How much do Pip and the reader now know about Miss Havisham and Estella? Perhaps more to the point, what is it that Pip really wants to ask Jaggers? Why should Jaggers avoid looking at Estella, and why should she often look at him? Is there an unspoken secret between them? Certainly it creates a mystery for Pip and the reader. Remember, this book was written as a serial, and all these questions will be answered later.

Estella

The surrounding of Estella with glittering jewels by Miss Havisham reminds us of the image of the inaccessible star, and of how Estella will keep Pip from Joe, as he admits in the final paragraph of the chapter.

Chapter 30

Pip speaks to Jaggers and brings about Orlick's dismissal. In the village Pip's enjoyment of his new status is spoiled by the mocking antics of Trabb's boy. Back in London,

Herbert and Pip confide in one another – Pip tells of his love for Estella and Herbert speaks of his love for Clara, the daughter of a retired ship's purser. They go to see Wopsle in a performance of 'Hamlet'.

Pip interferes

Pip is instrumental in Orlick's dismissal. Later he will have cause, perhaps, to regret the action.

The encounter with Trabb's boy is hilarious for us, but not for Pip. Even the repetition of 'Don't know yah!', which ought to have reminded Pip of the cruel way he had ignored Joe, leaves him untouched. His own dignity is so offended that he writes to Trabb's employer in an obvious effort to get him dismissed. You will appreciate the irony of this when you consider the later actions of Trabb's boy and those of the other person Pip has caused to be dismissed from a job on this visit to Satis House. If you can't make the connection, Chapter 53 will provide the answer!

Pip's and Herbert's loves contrasted

The conversation between Pip and Herbert is interesting because it is one of

Pip

the rare moments when Pip's current state of mind is explicitly discussed. Herbert gives sound reasons why Pip should give up Estella, and these are not rejected by Pip, since he already understands the truth of what is said to him. Compare Pip's overpowering, unrealistic compulsion to love and be socially acceptable to Estella with the reality of Herbert's love for his Clara, which is established through humour and lack of social pretension.

Chapter 31

Wopsle's play is farcical. Pip and Herbert visit Wopsle backstage and invite him home to dinner. That night, Pip has nightmares which confuse his expectations, hopes and aspirations.

Mr Waldengarver gives his Hamlet

Mr Wopsle, in various guises, provides a link between the stages of Pip's life.

Structure

He was with him when the convicts were re-captured on the marshes; later Compeyson will track Pip into the theatre where he is performing just before Magwitch's attempted escape. Here the playbill brought by Joe links Wopsle's past and present. His ludicrous attempt on Hamlet provides light relief as well as a parody of Pip's pretensions. In Victorian times it was not uncommon for amateurs to take leading Shakespearean roles in the professional theatre, often paying for the privilege.

See what humour you can find in the description of the staging, the performances and the views of the theatre aired by Mr Wopsle/Waldengarver and his dresser.

Examiner's tip

When you examine the theme of 'great expectations', you need to examine more characters than just Pip. Wopsle's expectations are ludicrous, founded on little more than his own vanity, but you should examine the playbill in Chapter 27 for a fine display of pomposity.

Chapter 32

A note from Estella announces her arrival in London and Pip, overjoyed, goes to meet her coach at Cheapside. While waiting, he meets Wemmick and accompanies him to Newgate Prison. The sordidness of the prison contrasts with Pip's vision of Estella. He feels a 'nameless shadow' when he sees Estella and ponders on the taint of crime which seems to surround him.

Pip at Newgate

The visit to Newgate should put us in mind of the still unsolved mystery of Magwitch. Also, be aware of how frequently events are duplicated. This is Pip's second visit to Newgate. Can you remember the circumstances of his first visit? Note how the ability to pay is the sole criterion of whether or not Wemmick will speak to someone. He sees nothing wrong with accepting gifts from prisoners and even requesting 'portable property' from condemned criminals.

Social aspects

Estella writes to Pip

Note the contrast between the cold tone of Estella's note and Pip's frantic response. There is irony in Pip's desire to rid himself of the air and dust of Newgate so as not to sully the 'proud and refined' Estella. The 'nameless shadow' which he mentions suggests there is a hidden secret about her past – time will tell, and illuminate the irony. Alternatively you could read ahead to Chapter 48.

Chapter 33

Pip travels to Richmond with Estella, whose behaviour suggests she is merely obeying orders. She tells Pip that he is to accompany her on various social occasions. She speaks of her dislike of the 'Toady' Pockets and enquires about Newgate and Jaggers.

Estella obeys her orders

'I am going to Richmond...' Note the absolute control which Miss Havisham seems to exert over these two young people, even to the extent that Estella puts her arm through Pip's 'as if it must be done'. Though Estella gives the impression of doing only what she has been ordered to do, you should be able to find some signs, not of affection for Pip (she still finds him a 'ridiculous boy' for kissing her hand), but of treating him more like an equal and of trusting his opinion.

Estella

The conversation about the Pocket family and their hatred for Pip gives a small insight into Estella's life at Satis House. It is ironic that Pip should worry lest their lies should do him a disservice in Miss Havisham's eyes, when his expectations from her are, in reality, without foundation.

The reference to Newgate prison and Estella's reaction: 'Wretches!', her mention of seeing Jaggers 'ever since I can remember', and her obvious dislike of the man are all highly ironic. She seems far removed from that world, yet her origins, life and fortune are inextricably bound up with them.

Chapter 34

Pip leads an idle and extravagant life. He and Herbert join a young men's club, The Finches of the Grove, of which Drummle is also a member. Pip and Herbert realise the need to sort out their finances. A formal letter from Trabb & Co tells Pip that Mrs Joe is dead.

Pip feels guilty

The recurring guilt which Pip feels about Joe and Biddy resurfaces, perhaps suggesting that he can be redeemed. Conflicting values in Pip's life – the warmth and vitality of Joe and the frigid attractions of Estella – are expressed by opposed imagery of fire and stars throughout the novel.

Pip

The lavish lifestyle of an idle gentleman has no purpose. It leads Pip towards debt and unsettles Herbert, and the membership of The Finches of the Grove will lead Pip into even greater excesses and highlight the Victorian view of what a 'gentleman' was.

Social class

The emptiness of social pretension and the lives of the idle rich are well summarised in the Finches of the Grove who 'spent their money foolishly' and aim for 'the present promotion of good feeling', only to eat vast meals and quarrel among themselves.

Herbert and Pip become depressed by their debts, and revive their flagging spirits by doing their 'book-keeping' in such a way as to pretend to themselves that they have money to spare: their 'margin'.

Announcement of Mrs Joe's death

The sudden intrusion of Pip's old life in the form of this brief, almost brutal letter announcing his sister's death and funeral, highlights the gulf that has opened between himself, Joe and Biddy.

Chapter 35

Pip is shocked by his sister's death, although he did not feel much love for her. He wonders about her attacker. The funeral is a mixture of farce and insensitivity. Biddy announces her intention of leaving the forge and complains that Orlick is still bothering her. Pip is angry when Biddy seems unconvinced by his promise to visit the forge regularly.

Mrs Joe's funeral – Biddy judges Pip

Pip's response to Mrs Joe's death is 'regret' without 'tenderness'. Notice the

way the sunshine and summer landscape at the funeral 'softens the edge' of his childhood fears of her. The funeral is made into an occasion of pretentiousness by onlookers and participants alike. Only Joe seems to be really upset and, when he voices the opinion that he would have preferred to carry her to church himself, he cuts through the social pretensions and we see his worth once again.

Pip's suggestion that Biddy ought to have written to him receives a sharp answer. If Pip had been more responsible, he might have bothered, from time to time, to enquire after his sister's health! Insensitive as ever, Pip offers her money but fails to realise that Biddy has changed from the girl he once knew into a mature woman. Her thoughts on what Pip has become are expressed clearly enough for us to understand that she would no more take money from him than Joe would take money from Jaggers in exchange for him. Biddy's remark later in the chapter, casting doubt on whether Pip will actually visit Joe, shows that her judgement of his character is shrewd.

A deathbed repentance?

What would appear to be a deathbed repentance on Mrs Joe's part, when she

asks for Joe's and Pip's pardon, finds a parallel later in a similar scene with Miss Havisham. Both women had a great influence on Pip's life: Mrs Joe in a negative and punitive way, depriving him of love and comfort in his childhood; Miss Havisham by giving him expectations which she knows he can never attain – or so she thinks. It is possible that both women repent for the same reason in recognising the wrong they have done him.

Sunshine and mist

The reference to Orlick and his threatening presence serves as a timely

reminder that his part in the story is yet to be told. Cross-references like this enable *Great Expectations* to proceed on interlocking paths as two types of novel: the first the story of Pip's growth to manhood, developing and then discarding false pretensions, and a mystery story, creating and then solving

Structure

such mysteries as the murder of Mrs Joe, the ancestry of Estella, the identity of Pip's benefactor and many more. And it is appropriate at this point that we should see Joe in bright light and sunshine, perhaps reflecting the future which lies in store for him – and Pip in mist, reflecting…what?

Chapter 36

Pip has his twenty-first birthday and Jaggers informs him that he will now have a yearly income of five hundred pounds. He will not tell Pip any more about his benefactor. Pip wants to help Herbert and consults Wemmick about it.

Jaggers shows that he is aware of Pip's lifestyle, but expresses no opinions on the matter, in keeping with the way he carries out his job. Jaggers' response to Pip's questions about his benefactor causes Pip to draw some foolish conclusions.

Walworth and Little Britain

Wemmick is an excellent example of Dickens' ability to build memorable minor characters around amusing and well-observed habits and speech patterns. The essential feature of Wemmick is his ability to keep private life and business separate, to the extent that his face re-sets itself as he moves between office and home. In this chapter note the references to 'portable property' and 'the Aged', the metaphor of the bridges and (as ever) the post office mouth. Wemmick, of course, has significant plot involvement and is used as a contrast to Jaggers, as well as being one of Dickens' gallery of eccentrics.

Characterisation

As a minor character Wemmick is nevertheless memorable, partly because Dickens creates his own little world, peopled by such innocents as the Aged Parent and Miss Skiffins. In addition, Wemmick has an important function in the plot and contributes to the theme of worldly success.

Chapter 37

At Walworth, Wemmick discusses Pip's plan for Herbert sympathetically and arranges for Pip to buy Herbert a partnership in a firm of shipbrokers. These arrangements are to be kept secret. Pip meets Miss Skiffins.

A contrast in love and Pip's first act of generosity

Wemmick's home and caring lifestyle remind the reader of Pip's neglect of Joe. The humorous account of Wemmick's courtship of Miss Skiffins provides a contrast to the coldness which greets Pip's unsuccessful attempts to carry on a love affair with Estella.

Through Wemmick, Pip arranges a place for Herbert in business; this will have useful consequences later in the novel. For so long the recipient of another's anonymous gifts, Pip now becomes an anonymous benefactor himself. It is perhaps his first real act of generosity though, ironically, made with money he received from his own benefactor.

Chapter 38

Pip becomes Estella's regular escort but is made jealous by her other suitors. She warns Pip that she is incapable of love and Miss Havisham too is caught in this trap. There is a quarrel between the two women. Drummle tells Pip that he knows Estella and Pip expresses disquiet that Estella should encourage such a worthless character. The chapter ends with a story about an impending threat which sums up Pip's predicament.

Estella

Pip often escorts Estella and we might wonder if her repeated warnings to him suggest a growing affection, or whether she is simply warning Pip that she cannot be held responsible for actions which might cause him serious harm. In Pip's final conversation with Estella in this section of the novel she makes her intentions clear, and Pip would not appear to be included in them.

Estella and Miss Havisham fall out

The quarrel between Estella and Miss Havisham comes as a surprise. Nowhere

Miss Havisham

has there been any indication that such a dispute might arise. However, note how perfectly Miss Havisham has been caught in her own trap. By teaching Estella to be cold and unfeeling she has at the same time excluded herself from the possibility of being loved by Estella, and has suddenly become aware that this is the very thing she wants most.

The Finches of the Grove

In the exchange with Drummle at the Finches of the Grove, Pip again shows an immature pomposity and punctiliousness, going so far as to propose a duel for the lady's good name (a knight in shining armour!), though soon dissuaded. However, his taking offence at Drummle is not surprising. There are many characters whose appearances are deceptive (Magwitch, notably); Drummle on every appearance is as boorish and unpleasant as he appears at first. Of which other character could this be said?

Chapter 39

Pip is now twenty-three and has heard nothing further about his 'expectations'. One stormy night he is receives a visit from a stranger whom he realises is Magwitch, the convict from his childhood. It is a great blow to Pip to learn that it is Magwitch, not Miss Havisham, who is his benefactor. Pip now knows that Miss Havisham has only been using him for her diversion and has never intended him for Estella. Worse still, he has neglected Joe in favour of 'expectations' which have, in reality, been paid for by a convict. Nonetheless Pip feels he owes it to Magwitch to give safe shelter to him.

Magwitch returns

Note how the oppressive atmosphere and stormy weather remind us of the marshes years before when Pip first met the convict. This is a fitting climate in which to reintroduce Magwitch. At last Pip learns the true source of his expectations, and the news is not welcome. When Magwitch finally claims due recognition for having made Pip a 'gentleman', Pip shrinks in fear and dread. We now see the convict in a new light: a man of his word, he fulfils the promise contained in the thoughtful look he gave Pip as he was being taken away to resume his captivity at the beginning of the novel.

As the second volume ends, the novel changes character again. Pip can no longer be deceived about Miss Havisham's intentions and he sees his relationship with many characters in a new light. Above all, the nature of the narrative is about to change. There has always been mystery; now violence and suspense accompany the thrills of the chase and the fears of the hunted.

■ Self-test questions Chapters 20–39 (Volume 2)

Uncover the plot
Delete two of the three alternatives given, to find the correct plot. Beware possible misconceptions and muddles.
Unimpressed by London, Pip meets his guardian ~~Wemmick~~/Jaggers/~~Mr Pocket~~ and observes his handling of his clients. He is then sent to ~~the Castle/the counting-~~

house/Barnard's Inn, the lodgings of Herbert/~~Matthew/Mike~~ Pocket. Recognising each other as the youthful boxers in Miss Havisham's garden, the two become friends and Pip learns Miss Havisham's story. Pip meets Herbert's ~~lawyers/guardians/~~parents and begins his studies. He dines with Wemmick, Jaggers' ~~client/~~clerk/~~confectioner~~, and shortly afterwards he and his fellow students Drummle and Startop/~~Flopson and Millers/Belinda and Molly~~ are invited to Jaggers' house. There, their attention is drawn to the strange housekeeper Molly/~~Mrs Coiler/Camilla~~. Drummle behaves badly and soon leaves Mr Pocket's/~~Jaggers'/ Wemmick's~~ tuition.

~~Biddy/~~Joe/~~Barnard~~ comes to London to tell Pip that Miss Havisham/~~Estella/Sarah Pocket~~ wants to see him. Pip travels back on a coach with two avengers/~~keepers~~/ prisoners; he recognises one of them as the stranger from the Three Jolly Bargemen/~~Miss Havisham's/the churchyard~~. At Miss Havisham's he is astonished to find that Orlick/~~the pale young gentleman/Trabb's boy~~ is the porter, and has him dismissed. Estella is ~~abroad/married/~~an elegant lady, but is unchanged in her manner to Pip. ~~Joe/~~Mrs Joe/~~Uncle Pumblechook~~ dies and Pip goes to the funeral. In London his debts mount up; ~~Wemmick/~~Jaggers/~~Matthew Pocket~~ informs him that he is to receive an annual sum of ~~£100/~~£500/~~£200~~, and he determines to use some of it to help Herbert/~~Drummle/Orlick~~. Estella and Miss Havisham quarrel; Drummle pursues ~~Jane/Biddy/~~Estella. Pip is ~~delighted/proud/~~horrified to learn that his benefactor is his convict, returned from exile to visit him.

Who? What? When? Why? How?

1 What does Jaggers mean when he says to the Jew: 'I am over the way'?
2 What does Herbert choose to call Pip, and what reason does he give?
3 Who, according to Herbert, was 'riotous, extravagant, undutiful – altogether bad'?
4 According to Herbert, at what time of day had Miss Havisham received her fiancé's letter – and how had Pip guessed this?
5 Who does Wemmick describe as 'a wild beast tamed'?
6 What is 'the Stinger'?
7 Who does Jaggers describe as 'the blotchy, sprawly, sulky fellow'?
8 Where were Molly's scars?
9 Who is the founder of Pip's fortunes, according to a local newspaper?
10 What does Pip believe Miss Havisham's intentions to be regarding himself and Estella?
11 Why is Estella going to Richmond?
12 Why does Pip perceive his influence to be harmful to Herbert?
13 When does Joe look 'natural, and like the Man he was'?
14 When does Jaggers say his part in Pip's affairs will be over?
15 How does Estella explain her coldness when accused by Miss Havisham?

Who is this?
Identify the following characters.
1 The pale young gentleman.
2 The 'prowling boy'.
3 The girl who is 'hard and haughty and capricious'.
4 The man who is reported to have said that 'no man who was not a true gentleman at heart, ever was…a true gentleman in manner.'
5 The man who says: 'Get hold of portable property.'
6 The man who says: 'for I really am not…an alarming personage'.
7 The Aged Parent
8 'Highly ornamental, but perfectly helpless and useless'
9 The man who is often to be found washing his hands.

10 A 'lively bright young fellow', 'exactly like his mother'.
11 'I have no softness there, no – sympathy – sentiment – nonsense'.
12 'He cross-examined his very wine when he had nothing else in hand.'
13 'He makes tremendous rows – roars, and pegs at the floor with some frightful instrument.'
14 '(He) walked among the prisoners much as a gardener might walk among his plants.'
15 '...there was something positively dreadful in the energy of her looks and embraces.'

Familiar themes
What important theme/image in the novel is being developed by the following lines/events?
1   To Mr Jaggers' fury, Mike says that his man is prepared to swear 'in a general way, anythink'.
2   'No varnish can hide the grain of the wood; and the more the varnish you put on, the more the grain will express itself.'
3   The recounting of Mrs Pocket's background.
4   'There we found, sitting by a fire, a very old man in a flannel coat; clean, cheerful, comfortable, and well cared for...'
5   The introduction of the Castle in Walworth, and Pip's observations of Wemmick's behaviour and manner there.

Open quotes
Complete the following.
1   'I had not been mistaken in my fancy that there was a simple dignity in him. The fashion of his dress...'
2   'At that time jails were much neglected...'
3   'We have no choice, you and I...'
4   'I would in preference have carried her to the church myself...'
5   'So...I must be taken as I have been made. The...'

Chapter 40

In the early morning, Pip stumbles over someone lurking on the staircase. Magwitch is to disguise himself as a farmer and use an assumed name – Provis. Pip moves him to lodgings in Essex Street. A visit to Jaggers verifies his benefactor's identity. Pip suffers alone for five days until Herbert's return. Magwitch swears Herbert to secrecy.

Pip thinks of others first – for once

With the notable exception of Herbert Pocket, it is a long while since Pip thought of anyone else before himself. But, suddenly, he loses interest in his 'great expectations' because of his growing concern for Magwitch's safety. As a transported criminal who has illegally returned to Britain, Magwitch is certain to be executed if caught. The contrast between his Australian safety and prosperity and his danger in London emphasises the

Pip

strength of his wish to see Pip a gentleman and places further responsibility on Pip not to reject him, a responsibility which Pip faces up to this time. Note the final irony of Magwitch informing Herbert that Pip will 'make a gentleman on you'.

When Magwitch makes Herbert take an oath of secrecy it is a reminder of his first meeting with Pip.

Chapter 41

Pip tells Herbert he is determined not to accept any more money from the convict. The two friends consider the effect of this on Magwitch and decide to get him out of England for his own safety. It is felt that Pip should leave England, too.

A new Pip starts to emerge

From now on, everything Magwitch says and does undermines Pip's social

Pip

pretensions and, in doing so, gradually releases Pip from the trap of false gentility. Having decided that he can accept no more money from Magwitch, Pip recognises the depths to which he has sunk: 'heavily in debt', 'no expectations', 'bred to no calling', 'fit for nothing'. The accuracy of Pip's analysis shows his growing self-awareness.

Herbert's offer to Pip of a job in the company in which he himself soon expects to become a partner is deeply ironic. As yet, Pip has not thought of the consequences for Herbert of his decision to reject Magwitch's money.

Chapter 42

Magwitch tells his story. Herbert informs Pip that Compeyson was Miss Havisham's lover and Arthur her half-brother.

This chapter begins to unravel some of the mysteries of the novel: the

Structure

relevance of the detailed story about Compeyson is not immediately obvious, but will become so and meanwhile, Compeyson is another example of a 'gentleman'; the gaps in the reader's knowledge about Miss Havisham are beginning to be filled; Magwitch's mysterious reference to a wife is significant in preparing us for the revelation of Estella's origins;

the identity of the other convict whom Magwitch pursued through the marsh is revealed, although we do not know his fate, and the disclosure moments later of his relationship with Miss Havisham must make the reader suspect that he will reappear.

Chapter 43

Pip realises Magwitch might be in danger from Compeyson. He feels he must visit Estella and Miss Havisham before going abroad. At the Blue Boar, Pip has an unpleasant encounter with Bentley Drummle, who is dining with Estella that night.

A tale of suspense

Although the development of Pip's character and the narration and solution of past mysteries are constant factors, the nature of the novel changes with each volume. At the end of Volume 1, Pip goes to London and the focus shifts. At the end of Volume 2 Magwitch returns. Apart from changing Pip's feelings about his 'great expectations', this transforms the narrative style. From the start there is the fear of capture (the lurking figure on the staircase, for instance) and Pip's life suddenly involves 'looking well about him' and 'night-consultations' about 'suspicious observation' and 'hazards'. The comedy and satire continue (as in the scene with Drummle), but in a setting of fear and suspense.

It is some while since we have seen Drummle. This incident serves to

Structure

refresh our minds about his character, reminds us of Pip's love for Estella, and is a comic satire on their 'gentlemanly' and ridiculous behaviour in disputing access to the warmth of the fire. The reference in the paragraph to Drummle's 'blundering brutal manner' with the horse will find its echo when we hear of the circumstances of his death, later in the story. At the end of the chapter, the shadowy figure of Orlick re-emerges.

Chapter 44

At Satis House, Pip confronts Miss Havisham and Estella. Miss Havisham admits her deception and Pip tells her of the virtues of Matthew and Herbert Pocket. He declares his love to Estella but she is unmoved and tells him she is to marry Drummle. Arriving back in London, Pip is warned by a note from Wemmick not to go to his rooms.

Pip at Satis House

We see a more assured Pip on this visit to Satis House. Note how he neatly turns Miss Havisham's dissuasive image 'what wind blows you here' to his own advantage. However, Pip's immediate purpose is to advance Herbert's cause, showing a growing generosity in his character.

Pip

Pip's impassioned declaration of love acknowledges that he realises that his cause is hopeless and provokes merely 'incredulous wonder' in Estella. What he achieves here (apart from interesting Miss Havisham on behalf of Herbert) is a frankness of understanding and an equality of position that have not been there before. An area of misunderstanding remains around Estella's view of love and marriage. Pip still cannot understand that her upbringing by Miss Havisham means that a suitable marriage for her is to someone she despises: 'Don't be afraid of my being a blessing to him.' Equally she cannot comprehend his 'sentiments, fancies'.

Returning to London

Pip's walking to London is unusual, though far from impossible. Dickens himself walked from London to Rochester (the site of Satis House), a distance of about 30 miles, one night in 1857 when he felt restless with stress. Pip is similarly disturbed. Note the end of the chapter (inevitably the end of a serial episode as well) for Dickens' use of suspense and mystery.

Chapter 45

Pip spends a bad night in Hummums Hotel and in the morning goes to Wemmick's home. Wemmick has heard that Compeyson is in London and that Pip's apartment is being watched. Wemmick suggests a plan to move Magwitch to the riverside house of Clara Barley, Herbert's fiancée, until he can be put on board a ship.

The Hummums, Walworth and the river

A sense of place is crucial to Dickens' effects in *Great Expectations*. The Hummums, so-called from being founded on the site of a Turkish bath, only encourages Pip's melancholy fantasies, but Walworth represents security and routine where Pip is recruited to toast the Aged's sausage (from Wemmick's own pig). Even here the conversation has to be of prison rumours, spies and a safe house for Magwitch. Examine Wemmick's conversation for signs of strict secrecy.

In many of Dickens' novels the River Thames plays a key part: after all, in the nineteenth century it was still a much more important means of transport into and around London than today. Herbert and Wemmick's choice of hiding place for Magwitch is by no means his first connection with the river: consider what part it has played in his life.

Chapter 46

Pip meets Herbert's Clara at her house. Magwitch is given a room at the top of the house and has softened in character. He agrees to leave England, so Pip and Herbert decide to go rowing regularly on the river in order to avoid suspicion later.

Pip learns from Herbert

In Pip's reaction to meeting Clara, there is evidence that he is developing a

realistic set of values. Note his comment near the end of this chapter when he refers to 'the redeeming youth and trust and hope' which marks Herbert's and Clara's relationship. There was no such feeling between himself and Estella. Note also the difference between Herbert's and Pip's view of the river,

Pip

which is determined by what it represents for each of them: for Pip, Magwitch and frustrated expectations; for Herbert, Clara and 'great expectations' of the future with her.

Chapter 47

During the weeks of waiting for an appropriate moment to get Magwitch away, Pip rows regularly on the river. He no longer uses Magwitch's money and is falling into debt. Pip learns that he is being followed by Compeyson and he informs Wemmick by letter.

The plot now focuses on the preparations for escape: there is less on Pip's social and personal life and, even when we have the entertainment of another theatrical disaster for Mr Wopsle, dark hints of the pursuit surface. Dickens provides a gloriously ridiculous account of farce and pantomime: at the time few theatres were licensed for 'straight' plays and such mixed bills were very popular. The mystery begins with the fixation of Wopsle's stare, apparently at Pip, but in reality at Compeyson who is dogging Pip's steps.

Chapter 48

Pip is dining with Wemmick and Jaggers when he receives a note from Miss Havisham, asking him to see her on business. Pip is suddenly aware of a resemblance between Jaggers' housekeeper Molly, and Estella. Wemmick tells Molly's life story to Pip on the way home. Pip learns that Molly once had a daughter.

The mystery of Estella and Molly explained

At last, Pip makes the connection between Estella and Molly, bringing final confirmation of the illusory nature of his expectations and dreams with regard to Estella. The account of Molly's trial adds another fragment to the detailed picture of those whose lives have touched on Pip's expectations.

Structure

Chapter 49

Pip visits Miss Havisham and, sensing her loneliness, feels pity for her. When he explains how he has set up Herbert in business but can no longer afford to do so, Miss Havisham agrees to pay the outstanding moneys out of her own pocket. Estella is now married to Drummle. As Pip leaves, his old vision of Miss Havisham hanging in the brewery returns and causes him to turn back. As he enters her room, he sees her dress catch fire and though he is able to save her, she is badly burned. Miss Havisham is placed on the great table. Delirious, she murmurs about remorse and forgiveness.

Satis House: reconciliation and inferno

The conversation between Miss Havisham and Pip shows two changed characters: Miss Havisham feels remorse for her treatment of Pip, and he pities her.

Miss Havisham repeats over and over again, 'What have I done?' Think about how she has damaged the lives of both Pip and Estella and note her changed relationship with Pip ('my Dear!'). How far did Miss Havisham's original intentions differ from what she has actually achieved? Miss Havisham herself knows nothing of the interlocking stories of herself, Estella, Molly and Magwitch, but what she tells Pip of Estella confirms the connections he is beginning to make.

> **Examiner's tip**
> Pip and Estella are required to work out the great expectations of Magwitch and Miss Havisham. For Pip events fail to take the desired course: think about whether any of the other three can be said to achieve what they planned or what was planned for them.

In endeavouring to put out the flames, Pip destroys the mouldering heap that was the wedding feast. The description of the insects fleeing from the fire and the blazing tinder of the wedding dress provide a grotesque finale to the Miss Havisham episodes. Remember the prophecy that Miss Havisham made about the table on one of Pip's early visits to Satis House. Note Pip's generosity in kissing the woman who has done so much to blight his life.

Chapter 50

Herbert tells Pip all he has learned from Magwitch. Magwitch once had a wife and child. The woman murdered her rival in a jealous brawl and threatened to kill their child too. Magwitch believes that she actually did this. Pip becomes convinced that Estella is Magwitch's daughter.

The final piece of the puzzle now comes to light: Magwitch is Estella's father. The hold that Compeyson had over Magwitch is also explained. Can you list the threads of the plot which have still to run their course?

You should also note Dickens' skill in linking together threads from different narrative strands. Miss Havisham's fire effectively rounds off her strand of the plot, but leads to Pip's burned hands and arm, which affect him in the episode which rounds off the Orlick plot, both of which events have considerable repercussions on his part in the final stages of the Magwitch plot.

Chapter 51

Pip confronts Jaggers with the truth about Estella's parentage, but Jaggers is reluctant to discuss it. With Wemmick's help, Pip extracts the full story. When Molly's case came to court, Jaggers placed her child in Miss Havisham's care and took Molly as his servant. Pip is warned never to tell Estella, as this knowledge would destroy her.

Pip confronts Jaggers

Note Pip's new self-assurance when he details his findings to Jaggers. Jaggers' attempt to regain control of the situation is overwhelmed by Pip's appeal for man-to-man frankness.

This chapter provides some much-needed light relief during this darker phase of the novel. Examine the amusing consequences of Pip's revealing Wemmick's secret: a pleasant home and an old father! Even the essential advice from Jaggers is relieved by his stress upon the 'imaginary' nature of these events, a parody of legal confidentiality.

Chapter 52

Herbert is soon to go to the East to a new branch of Clarriker's. Wemmick eventually sends word that the time is right to move Magwitch. Pip and Herbert plan to take him downriver in the rowing-boat and put him aboard the Hamburg steamer. Pip then receives an anonymous note telling him to go to the marshes where he will learn something about Provis (Magwitch). He visits Satis House and, avoiding the Blue Boar, dines at another inn, where he hears of Pumblechook's complaints of his 'ingratitude'. He finds he has lost the anonymous note.

Pip's pleasure in completing the arrangements for Herbert's partnership illustrate the extent to which he has redeemed himself from his self-centred way of life.

A further element of mystery is introduced by the note. His decision to go without telling anyone is perhaps foolhardy. The claims of the impostor Pumblechook make Pip recognise how much he owes to Joe and Biddy. Pip's heart is 'deeply and most deservedly humbled'.

Pip

Chapter 53

Orlick surprises Pip and tries to kill him. Herbert, who has found the note, arrives to save him. Pip returns to London and is soon well enough to continue with the plan for Magwitch's escape.

Orlick attempts murder

Orlick's attempt to murder Pip ties up more loose ends. Orlick is revealed as

the man who attacked Mrs Joe, as the intruder on the stairs of Pip's lodgings, and as a watcher in the shadows all the times that Pip was trying to protect Magwitch by disguising him. Confident that he is about to kill Pip, Orlick is careless of what he tells him, including his connection with Compeyson. The

Structure

fortuitous loss of Orlick's note brings Pip's friends to him and also brings Pip's old tormentor, Trabb's boy, who turns into an ally and is rewarded by a grateful Pip.

The return to the marsh with its wind and loneliness, puts us in mind of Pip's first visit, when he was threatened by the convict. For the first time in the novel, Pip seems to have lost his fear of the place.

Atmosphere

The omens for Magwitch's escape are not good. Though Herbert has rescued Pip from Orlick, he is left in terror of not being fit for the attempt, near-delirious, with burning and throbbing head and arm. Orlick's reference to Compeyson emphasises the danger he poses: it is difficult to share Herbert's cheerfulness.

Chapter 54

The escape party row downriver and spend the night at a riverside inn. There is news of a mysterious boat in the vicinity. Pip sees two strangers looking at his boat. The next morning the escape plan fails when a police boat intercepts them. Compeyson is the muffled figure aboard the police vessel. A steamer runs down Pip's boat and the two old enemies fight in the water. Compeyson is drowned but the badly wounded Magwitch, together with his money, is taken by the police. Pip accompanies him.

The river claims a victim

The river that brought the two convicts into Pip's life is now the scene of

their final meeting. The fight between them echoes their first conflict and brings the novel full circle.

Here we see Pip with all pretension stripped away, free to find his own standards of what is right and of value. Pip's monetary expectations are confiscated by the Crown, but he

Expectations

wants Magwitch to retain the illusion that his money has given Pip all that he wanted for him – another example of Pip's growing thoughtfulness towards others.

Much of the chapter is devoted to the complicated river journey by which Pip and his associates attempt to intercept the Hamburg or Rotterdam steamer near Gravesend. Dickens worked out a chart of the tides, and a similar interest in the authenticity of river life fills the whole chapter. With its details of bridges, shipping and riverside inns this picture of the Thames forms a vivid background to the cementing of the relationship between Pip and Magwitch.

Chapter 55

Magwitch's trial is set for a month later. Jaggers tells Pip there is no chance of acquittal or of recovering his money. Pip is offered work with Herbert, but delays his answer. Herbert leaves to take up his work out East and Clara will join him later. Wemmick explains that he was deliberately misinformed about Compeyson's whereabouts on the day of the escape. Wemmick marries Miss Skiffins in a humorously secretive ceremony. He does not want Jaggers to be informed.

Wemmick's marriage to Miss Skiffins is very humorously portrayed, as he acquires his most precious of 'portable properties'. But now both Pip's true companions, Herbert and Wemmick, are married. Pip is alone, far from Biddy and Joe, and Estella is also married. Pip's isolation is complete.

Chapter 56

Magwitch's condition worsens. He lies, uncomplaining, in the prison infirmary. Pip's daily visits create a loving bond between them. Magwitch is condemned to death, in company with thirty other criminals. But he dies before the day of execution. Pip's formal appeals for mercy prove fruitless, but Magwitch dies peacefully as Pip tells him his daughter is alive and is a beautiful lady, whom he loves.

The trial scene gives a chilling picture of 'justice' at work. Thirty-two men and women in the dock together receive the death sentence. There is no individual consideration, no humanity and no justice. Note Magwitch's dignity. Remember the 'bundle of shivers' and the monster from the 'distant savage lair'. Do you see either of them now?

Social aspects   Magwitch's last hours contain fine moments, and when Pip finally tells Magwitch that his daughter is alive and that Pip loves her, it makes a moving climax to their relationship.

Chapter 57

Pip, in considerable debt, falls into a delirious fever. Because of his condition, he avoids being sent to a debtors' prison. When, some weeks later, the delirium clears, Pip recognises his nurse as Joe. Joe, now able to write, sends word of Pip's recovery to Biddy. He tells Pip that Miss Havisham has died, leaving Matthew Pocket four thousand pounds in her will and only insulting amounts to the 'Toadies'. There is news of Orlick, too: he has been put in prison for burgling Pumblechook's shop. Joe is tactful and gentle but, as Pip recovers becomes increasingly respectful. Finally, he settles Pip's debts and leaves without a word. Pip decides to go to the forge to ask Joe to forgive him and Biddy to marry him.

Pip's illness brings Joe back into his life and his love for Joe becomes apparent. Note his cry: 'O Joe, you break my heart!' It is Joe's love which 'breaks' Pip, not his infatuation for Estella. Pip also realises what Joe really is: a 'gentle Christian man'.

Joe makes it obvious that he knows Pip's secrets regarding Magwitch, though he never refers specifically to names or incidents: his habit of 'supposing' is a less sophisticated-sounding version of Jaggers' 'Put the case...'. What faults of each of them are happily dismissed as 'onnecessary subjects'?

Joe Gargery

Characterisation

Dickens typically characterises from externals, but with Joe he works from the amusing details to create a three-dimensional character with an admirable philosophy of life (expressed sometimes in comically primitive terms). Note Joe's rationalisation of life with his first wife.

Gathering loose ends

The death of Miss Havisham and the details of her will with its setting-right of the wrongs done to Matthew Pocket and with the other Pockets getting their just deserts, neatly ties up a number of loose ends.

Orlick's arrest for housebreaking, and the humiliation of Pumblechook whose house it was he broke into, neatly brings their part in the story to an end – although you might wonder if Orlick is sufficiently punished for attacking Mrs Joe and Pip!

Chapter 58

Satis House is to be sold and pulled down. At the Blue Boar, Pumblechook begins patronising Pip again. In the village, Biddy's school is closed and, on arriving at the forge, Pip is amazed to find Biddy and Joe celebrating their wedding day. Pip asks them to forgive him his past behaviour, and they say emotional farewells. Pip joins Herbert and Clara in the East. He lives happily, writes regularly to Joe and Biddy and, over the years, pays off his debts. The secret of the origins of Herbert's partnership comes out. Herbert and Pip prosper, through honest hard work.

Pip's improved judgement of human worth shows in his increased respect for people such as Joe and Biddy, but also in his willingness to treat Pumblechook publicly with the scorn he deserves.

Despite his new awareness of Biddy's qualities he seems to have taken for granted that she will agree to marry him, so his latest expectations again come to nothing. All, however, is for the best. Joe and Biddy share the happiness they deserve; Pip is thankful to be spared the embarrassment of revealing his

Expectations

intentions; ironically, Pip's failed proposal leaves him free to be reunited with Estella.

Chapter 59

After eleven years in the East, Pip returns to the forge. Joe and Biddy's young son, also named Pip, reminds Pip of himself when young. He makes a sentimental visit to the grounds of Satis House. He meets Estella, now widowed and changed by her years of unhappy marriage. She asks Pip's forgiveness, he takes her by the hand, and they leave the ruined garden together.

An epilogue?

The final chapter in many Victorian novels is detached in time from the main narrative. Often this takes the form of a summary of the later careers of all the main characters; here it is one series of events from eleven years later. The upbringing of young Pip provides an illustration of a happy loving family seldom seen in the novel. The meeting of Pip and Estella, in the garden of the now-demolished Satis House with the stars shining through the mist, lays all the old ghosts to rest. Wisely and movingly the novel ends on Pip's conviction that they will not part, without the certainties of courtship or ceremony.

Social class

No doubt Dickens was partly moved to choose this ending by his reading public who wanted Pip and Estella to be reconciled, but you should note the effective way in which he renders social class irrelevant: Pip works 'pretty hard' to 'do well' and Estella finds this admirable.

A suitable ending?

Estella

Given what is known about Estella's character and life-story, is this ending appropriate? It was not Dickens' first choice. In the original form of the novel Estella re-marries (to a Shropshire doctor) after Drummle's death and Pip meets her once only, very briefly, in London. Young Pip is with him and she supposes Pip to be married and a father. After a brief conversation, the novel ends, '...she gave me the assurance that suffering had been stronger than Miss Havisham's teaching and had given her a heart to understand what my heart used to be.' Dickens was unsure which ending was better, though convinced that the changed one would be 'more acceptable'. Which one do you think is more suitable? Think about the psychology of the characters and also the mood and atmosphere of the novel.

■ Self-test questions Chapters 40–59 (Volume 3)

Uncover the plot

Delete two of the three alternatives given, to find the correct plot. Beware possible misconceptions and muddles.

Magwitch tells his story, in which Miss Havisham's lover is revealed to be the other convict Compeyson/~~Arthur/Jaggers~~. Pip learns that ~~Biddy~~/Estella/~~Molly~~ is to be married to Drummle, and that Magwitch and ~~Miss Havisham~~/Molly and ~~Jaggers/Molly~~-and Magwitch are Estella's parents. Miss Havisham repents, pays for Herbert's/~~Pip's/Magwitch's~~ partnership and is mortally injured in a fire. Pip, narrowly escaping death at the hands of Orlick/~~Trabb's boy/Arthur~~, undertakes to transport Magwitch to safety, but they are caught; Magwitch is mortally wounded and ~~Orlick/Pip/~~Compeyson killed. After Magwitch's death/~~execution/release~~, Pip falls ill and is reunited with Joe. Biddy and Joe are married and Satis House ~~burned/rebuilt~~/sold. Pip becomes a clerk/~~blacksmith/lawyer~~ with Clarriker and Co, returning years later to be reunited with Estella.

Who? What? When? Why? How?

1   What new identity does Pip give Magwitch, and what name does Magwitch himself assume?
2   Why does Pip have to disguise and conceal the convict?
3   Where do Herbert and Pip determine that Magwitch should go?
4   Who is the lady in white who haunts Arthur's death-bed?
5   Who does Wemmick mean by 'Tom, Jack or Richard'?
6   What word does Pip use repeatedly to describe the altered condition of Magwitch?
7   Where is Compeyson spotted, and by whom?
8   Who does Orlick refer to when he speaks of 'new companions, and new masters'?
9   What is to happen to Magwitch's wealth after his conviction?
10 When does Pip tell Magwitch about Estella?

Who is this?

1   '...as he turned his food in his mouth...he looked terribly like a hungry old dog.'
2   'He set up fur a gentleman...and he'd been to a public boarding-house and had learning'.
3   'He was in a Decline, and was a shadow to look at.'
4   '...in shutting out the light of day, she had shut out infinitely more'.
5   '...the woman was a young woman, and a jealous woman, and a revengeful woman'.
6   'His enjoyment of the spectacle I furnished...had malignity in it that made me tremble.'
7   '...a man who had felt affectionately, gratefully and generously...with great constancy'.
8   'He extended his hand with a magnificently forgiving air'.
9   'I had heard of her as leading a most unhappy life'.
10 'The freshness of her beauty was indeed gone'.

What weather?
Throughout the novel, and particularly in this section, Dickens uses the weather/night and day metaphorically and symbolically to create mood and character. With this in mind, answer the following questions.

1   How does Pip describe the day when he sets off for Satis House in Chapter 43?

2   How does Pip use the weather in his long speech to Estella beginning: 'Out of my thoughts!', and what effect does it have?

3   According to Pip, as he reflects upon Miss Havisham's past and actions on his last visit, what qualities does the daylight embody?

4   In his powerful courtroom description (56), what does the ray of sunlight do, and of what does Pip think it might remind the audience?

How to write a coursework essay

Most of you will use your study of *Great Expectations* as part of a Wide Reading coursework assignment for GCSE English/English Literature. If we look at the requirement of the NEAB examinations, we find that this assignment must involve *comparison* between a complete pre-twentieth-century prose text and a suitable twentieth-century text. It is also essential to make certain comments on the historical, social and cultural background to the texts. In the case of any Dickens novel, social issues are so much to the forefront that any essay, even one on character or plot, is likely to involve consideration of them. In the case of *Great Expectations* Pip's progress through the class system provides many examples that you could use in your assignment. Throughout the **Text commentary** the **Essays icon** draws attention to useful material for these assignments.

There are, of course, some general principles for these assignments.

Comparison is essential. No credit is given for telling the story of all or part of *Great Expectations* and that of a twentieth-century story with a vaguely similar theme. It is essential that you show that, while Dickens' presentation of childhood or class has a certain effect, your twentieth-century author affects the reader totally differently, in the same way or in a partially similar way.

Though comparison is essential, it is not required that you devote an equal amount of your essay to each of the texts. Similarly, there is no requirement that your twentieth-century comparative text is another novel: short stories, plays and poems are acceptable, and the only restriction is that the text 'must be of sufficient substance and quality to merit serious study'.

Your choice of twentieth-century comparative text is important. There must be specific grounds for comparison. This can, of course, mean that the twentieth-century story or novel is opposite in effect from Dickens: using similar ideas differently is a good ground for comparison, as, too, is obtaining comparable effects by different means.

The *most important consideration* in writing the essay is that it must develop an argument or explain a point of view consistently throughout. Choosing a title matters: if you write an essay called 'Growing up in *Great Expectations*' and *Joby*, you are not directing yourself towards a specific comparison. The comparison should be made throughout the essay, not necessarily in the same sentence, but at least in adjacent paragraphs. Careful advance planning will aid you in organising your theme or argument: making notes on the material, putting these notes in order, then working through two or three drafts of the essay. Thus you should be able to make a decision on what each paragraph is about, as far as possible signalling that to the reader in the opening sentence, often called a *topic sentence* because it states the topic of the paragraph.

In terms of length of essay, do bear in mind that it is only one of several pieces of coursework and there is no need for a 5,000 word blockbuster. Many essays will exceed 1,000 words: by how much depends on the material you wish to present and the advice of your teacher.

Social class

Give an account of the ways in which Dickens presents the issue of social class in Great Expectations, *considering what criticisms he makes of the class system and what forms of behaviour he finds admirable. Compare his views with those of Harold Brighouse in* Hobson's Choice.

The choice of twentieth-century comparison reminds you that it is not compulsory to choose a novel. In addition, *Hobson's Choice* is a text that you may be studying for GCSE English Literature (Twentieth-century Drama). Another possible choice in the same category is JB Priestley's *An Inspector Calls*.

You might wish to make the initial point that *Great Expectations* contains very little social criticism on Dickens' typical issues: poverty, child labour, education, etc. His attack on poor education (Mr Wopsle's great aunt) is brief and fairly mild, no central characters are notably poor or ill-housed, and many of the poorer characters are disreputable or criminal.

The essay is fairly straightforward and many of the issues are dealt with under **Expectations** in the **Themes and images** section of this book. Perhaps we should start with the ludicrous and generally held ideas that social acceptability and higher class depend upon not having to work. Dickens, a workaholic himself, admires people who make their way by their own efforts: Pip is at his most worthless when he does nothing but cultivate 'gentlemanly' ways and despise common people. The same view can be found to a large extent in the smaller world of Brighouse's Salford. Alice and Vicky expect middle-class comfort to come to them of right: the sympathies of the playwright are with the active Maggie who rises in the world by hard work and by being prepared to risk social disgrace (marrying the boothand Willie Mossop).

What Harold Brighouse mocks in the down-to-earth lower-middle-class world of *Hobson's Choice* is 'putting on airs'. Dickens' view of class is more complicated, worked out at much greater length, but ultimately not too different. You must examine the issue: 'What is a gentleman?'. This is dealt with in detail in this guide. There is no evidence that Dickens objects to prosperity or social position (Joe Gargery may be an ideal of goodness and generosity, but Pip has to take a wider view of the world), but he attacks the false standards that elevate breeding or riches above all else. You will find examples in profusion, such as the boorish gentleman Drummle (who obtains Estella), Mrs Pocket's pretensions, Magwitch's false dreams for Pip, and many more.

An important section of your essay will show how Dickens uses Pip's expectations of social advancement to reveal false standards in him and in others around him. This can be contrasted with Maggie's clear-eyed progress in *Hobson's Choice*, and her contempt for the false niceties of the class system. A particularly interesting comparison to be made is between the roles of Miss Havisham and Mrs Hepworth. Though she is nothing like Miss Havisham as a character, Mrs Hepworth's superior social position means that she receives the same grovelling obedience from Hobson as Miss Havisham does from Pumblechook. She then becomes the mysterious benefactor of Will and Maggie, though on terms that are well understood and agreed to, a neat contrast to Pip's situation.

This essay is likely to contain more material on *Great Expectations* than on *Hobson's Choice*, but you could round it off by reminding the reader of those respects in which they are similar, such as the respect for character and achievement rather than breeding and social position.

Childhood

The first volume of Great Expectations *is one of Dickens' most vivid presentations of growing up. What means does he use to make it so effective? Compare it to the picture of childhood drawn by Stan Barstow in* Joby.

Joby may at first sight appear an odd choice to compare with *Great Expectations*, and there is no doubt that it is a much less ambitious novel, but you will find that Pip and Joby have several features in common which you might like to compare for the first stage of your assignment. Each of them misunderstands the adult world; each of them dreams, with no justification, of a girl who is 'above' him; each is to be cut off from old associates, Joby by education, Pip in part by education, but mainly by acquaintance and expectations. Perhaps the key comparison is in regard to parents: the opening of *Great Expectations* tells of Pip's loss of parents, the opening of *Joby* tells of his fear of losing his mother and, later, he has to face up to the possible loss of his father, though not through death.

Dickens has a rare ability to return to a child's view of the world, helped in this novel by a first person narration which is poised between the viewpoint of Pip the adult and Pip the boy. Thus the narration is particularly convincing in that we can share Pip's confusion without being confused ourselves. This explaining of the boy's reasoning (as, for instance, when he tries to make sense of the appearance of the second convict) is a major factor in convincing the reader. The vividness of the account is aided by the mix of everyday occurrences (study/work at the forge) with remarkable adventures (Magwitch/Miss Havisham) to which Pip reacts in a wholly convincing way: even the lies about Miss Havisham have their origin in childish logic. Perhaps Dickens' finest effect is in surrounding the small Pip with larger-than-life characters (Magwitch/Pumblechook/Mrs Joe/Miss Havisham) who frighten or oppress him.

Nothing on this scale occurs in *Joby*. There is very much the same attempt to make sense of the world, but it is shown far more in dealings with his contemporaries. Joby, like Pip, is led astray, but for very different reasons. Like Pip, too, he becomes affected by a sense of guilt. The larger-than-life adults and the remarkable adventures are not there, but both novels have the same sort of moral centre: Joby and Pip have to decide what sort of people they want to be and to separate false friends from true.

Joby is set so precisely in time (July/August 1939) that a section on the social/historical background of the two novels would be helpful and not difficult to find material for.

An essential difference of technique (which you might like to make the concluding section of your essay) lies in Dickens' typically leisurely approach. In most of his novels he delights in showing the effect of years: characters and stories develop slowly, with the occasional sudden burst or transformation, within a comprehensive social picture. Stan Barstow, on the other hand, prepares the ground well (the prospect of war, the progress to grammar school, his mother's illness) and then makes Joby grow up suddenly in the space of one summer holiday. Other books that you might have studied and which you could use for this assignment instead of *Joby* also use this technique of focusing on a brief period of time full of problems for the central character(s): *A Kestrel for a Knave* and *To Kill a Mockingbird* are both suitable comparisons.

Characterisation

Examine the range and vividness of Dickens' characterisation in Great Expectations. *You should deal with the variety of methods used to create characters and how convincing you find them. Compare and contrast Dickens' methods of characterisation with Graham Greene's in* Brighton Rock.

It is very difficult to think of a twentieth-century equivalent of Dickens in terms of vitality and energy of characterisation. A novel which would make an excellent comparison, but is extremely demanding for a GCSE student, is Joseph Heller's *Catch 22*. Only the most ambitious of readers should attempt a novel which contains a Dickensian array of obsessives and eccentrics and the same glorious mix of comedy and menace. Such relish for bizarre characters is also to be found in novels outside the main stream which make no pretence at reality, science fiction/fantasy perhaps.

Graham Greene's *Brighton Rock* is certainly a worthwhile comparison, an excellent thriller in which the central characters are plagued as much by their moral weaknesses as by the mystery and danger of violence that underlies the whole novel.

Whatever the twentieth-century example you choose, a major part of the assignment is to examine Dickens' characterisation. You are asked to examine 'range'. This is great in whatever terms you take: in the levels of society of the characters, in their moral impact, in the naturalism or otherwise of their portrayals. Some characters convince more through the consistency and vigour of their creation than because we think there really are people like that: Pumblechook, for instance, an inspired caricature. Note the ways in which Dickens makes first appearances dramatic: Magwitch, obviously, but also Jaggers, Miss Havisham, Herbert and many more. Dialogue is the key to much of the characterisation. Some of the more two-dimensional characters (Wemmick, for instance) are brought to life by regularly repeated phrases. In characters of more weight (like Joe) these extend into patterns of speech. Some have the opportunity to tell their own story or present their own version of events.

The first difference that strikes the reader in *Brighton Rock* is the deliberate drabness of the characters: the pubs and race-courses of Brighton between the wars contain menace more than excitement and the people blend into the depressing background. You will, though, find the mixture of the ordinary and the evil that you also find in *Great Expectations*: Orlick attempting murder in the lime-kiln or Wemmick leaving warning notes would be well at home in Graham Greene's world. The other two essential differences in the characterisation of *Brighton Rock* are inter-linked. Dickens is a master of the creation of character from outside (his first person narrators like Pip being an exception). Greene takes us into the doubts and fears of all his main characters: the novel first reveals the thoughts and actions of a character (Hale) who is soon to die, then examines the consciences of Ida and Pinkie and ends with Rose's confession. This leads to the second main difference: *Brighton Rock* is a Catholic novel about Catholics and, where Pip may be plagued by guilt, Greene's characters never escape from sin.

The sort of conclusion you draw will depend on the choice of twentieth-century comparison, but one element in it is likely to be that Dickens is unmatched for the vigour, range and (sometimes) grotesqueness of his creations.

■ How to write an examination essay

Though most of you will be required to write on *Great Expectations* as part of your coursework, some of you may need to answer an examination question on it. This section considers one specific title on the novel, but also gives general advice on how to approach an English Literature essay.

Unlike many of Dickens' novels, Great Expectations *is not given the name of its central character as a title. Examine how the theme of 'great expectations' influences the whole of the novel, not only the character of Pip. You will need to consider which characters fulfil their expectations and what effect the expectations have on them.*

Before you start writing

- The first essential is thorough revision. It is important that you realise that even Open Book examinations require close textual knowledge. You will have time to look up quotations and references, but *only if you know where to look.*

- Read the questions very carefully, both to choose the best one and to take note of exactly what you are asked to do.

- Do not answer the question you *imagine or hope* has been set. In the case of the title we are considering, you are asked to examine the theme of 'great expectations' throughout the novel. Therefore, examining the effect that, firstly, Miss Havisham and Estella and, secondly, Magwitch's generosity, have on Pip will gain you some credit, but it is only part of the essay. The first stage of preparation is to think how many characters have great expectations and what comes of them.

- Identify all the key words in the question that mention characters, events and themes, and instructions as to what to do, e.g. compare, contrast, comment, give an account, etc. Write a short list of the things you have to do. In this case 'examine' and 'consider' are fairly general words, though with rather different meanings: 'examine' implies the search for evidence, 'consider' suggests thinking about the evidence you have found. Other key words are 'fulfil' and 'effect': you are not just to find examples of the widespread use of 'great expectations', but to see who carries them out (very few) and how the expectations change them (mostly for the worse).

- Look at the points you have identified and jot down what you are going to say about each. You will need to decide, for instance, how far you will deal with Magwitch's expectations separately from Pip's.

Writing the essay

- The first sentences are important. Try to summarise your response to the question so the examiner has some idea of how you plan to approach it. For example, 'The plot of the novel revolves around the effect that the protagonist, Pip's, great expectations have on his character and actions, but it would be a mistake to regard him as the only character to be affected in this way.' Jump straight into the essay; do not nibble at the edges for a page and a half. A personal response is rewarded, but you must always answer the question - as you write your essay, *refer back* to your list of points.

- Answer *all* of the question. Many students spend all their time answering just one part of a question and ignoring the rest. This prevents you gaining marks for the parts left out. In the same way, failing to answer enough questions on the examination is a waste of marks which can always be gained most easily at the start of an answer.

- There is no 'correct' length for an essay. What you must do is to spend the full time usefully in answering all parts of the question: spending longer than the allocated time by more than a few minutes is dangerous. It is an advantage if you can organise your time so well as to reach an elegant conclusion (perhaps on Dickens' attack on materialism), but it is better to leave an essay without a conclusion than to fail to start the next question.

- Take care with presentation, spelling and punctuation. It generally unwise to use slang or contractions (e.g. 'they've' for 'they have').

- Use quotation or paraphrase when it is relevant and contributes to the quality and clarity of your answer. References to events often do not need quotation, but you would probably need the exact words of, for instance, some of Jaggers' pronouncements or the conversations of Pip and Magwitch late in the novel. *Extended* quotations are usually unhelpful and are often used as padding, which is a complete waste of time.

Self-test answers Chapters 1–19 (Volume 1)

Uncover the plot

Pip, an orphan living with his sister, is frightened by an escaped convict into bringing a file and some food to the Battery. He does so, at first mistaking his convict for another. Christmas dinner is interrupted by soldiers, and Pip and Joe join the hunt for and arrest of the escaped prisoners. Pip is invited to play at Miss Havisham's, and meets the insulting Estella. Later, he calls in at the Three Jolly Bargemen and meets a stranger, who stirs his drink with a file and gives Pip a shilling wrapped in two one-pound notes.

Pip's visits to Miss Havisham's become regular. Joe brings Pip's indentures to Satis house and Pip is apprenticed; he is growing increasingly ashamed of his home and profession. Joe's journeyman Orlick is resentful when Pip takes a holiday to see Miss Havisham – only to learn that Estella is abroad. Mrs Joe is viciously attacked and Biddy moves in. Pip confesses his admiration of Estella and his hopes of becoming a gentleman. Pip learns from Mr Jaggers, a lawyer, that he has a benefactor from whom he will receive property and an education. Suspecting his benefactor to be Miss Havisham, he leaves for London.

Who? What? When? Why? How?

1   Pip's mother (1)
2   Pins and needles (2)
3   Uncle; corn-chandler (4)
4   At the bottom of a ditch, fighting (5)
5   To 'play' (7, 8)
6   On the dressing-table; yellow, and never worn (8)
7   Convinced that both he and Miss Havisham should not be understood; that it would be 'coarse and treacherous' to Miss Havisham and Estella to do so (9)
8   A file; it was Joe's file, that Pip had stolen for the convict (10)
9   Mr Jaggers, a lawyer (10)
10   A bride-cake (11)
11   On the long table, when she is dead (11)
12   Pip is to be apprenticed (12)
13   Dolge (15)
14   '…she was not worth gaining over.' (17)
15   He must keep his name, and not inquire as to the identity of his benefactor (18)

Who is this?

1   Pip (1)
2   Pip's convict (1)
3   Mrs Joe (2)
4   Joe, of his father (7)
5   Pip's convict (5)
6   Miss Havisham (8)
7   Miss Havisham, to Estella (8)
8   Estella (8)
9   Uncle Pumblechook (9)
10   Joe (9)
11   Herbert Pocket, the 'pale young gentleman' Pip fights (11)
12   Orlick (15)
13   Mrs Joe (15)

14 Biddy (17)

15 Uncle Pumblechook (19)

Familiar themes

1 Clothes do not make a person; what is inside is more important

2 People using other people for their own ends

3 Fellow humanity; the importance of compassion, even for sinners

4 Others can make you dissatisfied with yourself and turn away from your true nature; children are impressionable (compare Miss Havisham's manipulation of Estella)

5 Estella is beautiful like a star, but cold and inaccessible (like Pip's ambitions – compare with the images of fire and warmth used to describe Joe and the forge)

On the other hand

1 'She was not a good-looking woman, my sister...' (2)

2 To '...prevent some persons laying under suspicion alonger (him)' (5)

3 '...he hammered away at my mother, most onmerciful.' (7)

4 'I feel convinced that...I should not be understood.' (9)

5 'You're oncommon small. Likewise you're an oncommon scholar.' (9)

Like what?

1 Camilla, one of Miss Havisham's toady relations; a generally unpleasant appearance and character (11)

2 Joe's hand upon Pip's shoulder; his strength and his gentleness (17)

3 Mr Jaggers' words, to impress upon Joe the virtue of consistency; the lawyer's persuasive and somewhat pompous way with language (18)

4 Mr Jaggers' mannerism; his impressive but 'bull-baiting' manner (18)

5 Pip's dreams of 'doing something' for his village; a humorous perspective on his own inflated behaviour (19)

▣ Self-test answers Chapters 20–39 (Volume 2)

Uncover the plot

Unimpressed by London, Pip meets his guardian Jaggers and observes his handling of his clients. He is then sent to Barnard's Inn, the lodgings of Herbert Pocket. Recognising each other as the youthful boxers in Miss Havisham's garden, the two become friends and Pip learns Miss Havisham's story. Pip meets Herbert's parents and begins his studies. He dines with Wemmick, Jaggers' clerk, and shortly afterwards he and his fellow students Drummle and Startop are invited to Jaggers' house. There, their attention is drawn to the strange housekeeper Molly; Drummle behaves badly and soon leaves Mr Pocket's tuition.

Joe comes to London to tell Pip that Miss Havisham wants to see him. Pip travels back on a coach with two prisoners; he recognises one of them as the stranger from the Three Jolly Bargemen. At Miss Havisham's he is astonished to find that Orlick is the porter, and has him dismissed. Estella is an elegant lady but is unchanged in her manner to Pip. Mrs Joe dies and Pip goes to the funeral. In London his debts mount up; Jaggers informs him that he is to receive an annual sum of £500, and he determines to use some of it to help Herbert. Estella and Miss Havisham quarrel; Drummle pursues Estella. Pip is horrified to learn that his benefactor is his convict, returned from exile to visit him.

Who? What? When? Why? How?
1 He is acting for the other side, i.e. against the Jew's brother (20)
2 Handel; because of the Harmonious Blacksmith – 'We are so harmonious, and you have been a blacksmith' (22)
3 Miss Havisham's half-brother (22)
4 At twenty minutes to nine; all the clocks in Satis House had stopped at the same time (22)
5 Molly, Jaggers' housekeeper (24)
6 The gun at Wemmick's Walworth property (25)
7 Bentley Drummle (26)
8 On her wrists (26)
9 Uncle Pumblechook (28)
10 To bring them together (29)
11 To be shown to people and have people shown to her (33)
12 He is leading Herbert into debt (34)
13 In his working dress in the forge (35)
14 When Pip's benefactor discloses him/herself (36)
15 She is what Miss Havisham has made her (38)

Who is this?
1 Herbert Pocket (21)
2 Pip (21)
3 Estella (22)
4 Herbert's father, Matthew Pocket (22)
5 Wemmick (24)
6 Mr Pocket (23)
7 Wemmick's father (25)
8 Mrs Pocket (23)
9 Jaggers (26)
10 Startop (25, 26)
11 Estella (29)
12 Jaggers (29)
13 Clara's father (30)
14 Wemmick (32)
15 Miss Havisham (38)

Familiar themes
1 Corruption in the legal system (20)
2 A gentleman at heart will also be a gentleman in manner; appearance and reality; the blinding effect of ignorance and prejudice (22)
3 Social ambitions and expectations; the harm they can cause impressionable children (23)
4 The importance of love, humanity and compassion (compare with Pip's treatment of Joe) (25)
5 The difference between the public and the private man (25)

Open quotes
1 'could…no more come in its way when he spoke these words, than it could come in its way in Heaven.'
2 '…and the period of exaggerated reaction consequent on all public wrong-doing – and which is always its heaviest and longest punishment – was still far off.'
3 '…but to obey our instructions.'
4 '…along with three or four friendly ones wot come to it with willing harts and arms.'
5 'success is not mine, the failure is not mine, but the two together make me.'

Self-test answers Chapters 40–59 (Volume 3)

Uncover the plot
Magwitch tells his story, in which Miss Havisham's lover is revealed to be the other convict Compeyson. Pip learns that Estella is to be married to Drummle, and that Molly and Magwitch are Estella's parents. Miss Havisham repents, pays for Herbert's partnership and is mortally injured in a fire. Pip, narrowly escaping death at the hands of Orlick, undertakes to transport Magwitch to safety, but they are caught; Magwitch is mortally wounded and Compeyson killed. After Magwitch's death, Pip falls ill and is reunited with Joe. Biddy and Joe are married and Satis House sold. Pip becomes a clerk with Clarriker and Co, returning years later to be reunited with Estella.

Who? What? When? Why? How?
1   His uncle; Provis (40)
2   Because the convict would be sentenced to death if he were caught having returned from exile (40)
3   Out of England (41)
4   Miss Havisham (42)
5   Magwitch (45)
6   Softened (46)
7   Behind Pip at the theatre; by Mr Wopsle (47)]
8   Compeyson (53)
9   Forfeited to the crown (54)
10 Just before he dies (55)

Who is this?
1   Magwitch (40)
2   Compeyson (42)
3   Arthur, Miss Havisham's half-brother (42)
4   Miss Havisham (49)
5   Molly, Estella's mother (50)
6   Orlick (53)
7   Magwitch (54)
8   Pumblechook (58)
9   Estella (59)
10 Estella (59)

What weather?
1   '...creeping on, halting and whimpering and shivering...like a beggar' (43)
2   To show how she has been essential to every part of his life ('in the light, in the darkness'); it is very powerful and moving (44)
3   All that is natural and healthy (49)
4   Links the Judge and the condemned; that everyone passes on, absolutely equal, to a greater judgement that cannot be faulty (56)

Natasha will conclude
with a hairstyle consisting
of an extravagant style
created from each race

Mum, it is ~~some~~ a producer
from YCT.V

IS she Black

Yes ☐   NO ☑

aslan

she
doesn't
even know
what she's
doing;
can't spell
nothing?

Are you sure
she is a
producer?

Yes,
positive